Dedication

We dedicate this research to the improvement
of the language and literacy of

Max, Taylor, Abigail, Riley, Daniel, Charlotte

and to

Mairin, Claire, Jake, Colm, Senan

and to the boys and girls who participated in this study and
to all other little boys and girls and their families.

Family Literacy Matters: A Longitudinal Parent-Child Literacy Intervention Study

Linda M. Phillips
Canadian Centre for Research on Literacy
Ruth Hayden
Canadian Centre for Research on Literacy
Stephen P. Norris
Centre for Research in Youth, Science Teaching and Learning

Faculty of Education
University of Alberta

DETSELIG
ENTERPRISES LTD

Calgary, Alberta, Canada

Family Literacy Matters

©2006 Linda M. Phillips, Ruth Hayden, and Stephen P. Norris

Library and Archives Canada Cataloguing in Publication

Phillips, Linda, 1952-
   Family literacy matters : a longitudinal parent-child literacy intervention study / Linda M. Phillips, Ruth Hayden, Stephen Norris.

Includes bibliographical references and index.
ISBN-13: 978-1-55059-339-6
ISBN-10: 1-55059-339-0

   1. Family literacy programs. I. Hayden, Ruth II. Norris, Stephen P. (Stephen Patrick), 1949- III. Title

LC149.P48 2006   302.2'244   C2006-905074-0

Detselig Enterprises Ltd.
210, 1220 Kensington Road NW
Calgary, Alberta, Canada T2N 3P5

Phone (403) 283-0900
Fax: (403) 283-6947
Email: temeron@telusplanet.net
www.temerondetselig.com

All rights reserved. No part of this book may be reproduced in any form or by any means without permission in writing from the publisher.

We acknowledge the support of the Government of Canada through the Book Publishing Industry Development Program (BPIDP) for our publishing program.

We also acknowledge the support of the Alberta Foundation for the Arts for our publishing program.

ISBN 1-55059-339-0   ISBN 978-1-55059-339-6   SAN 113-0234

Printed in Canada   Cover design by Alvin Choong

Contents

1. Introduction 11
2. Review of Relevant Literature 13
   What is Family Literacy? 13
   Historical Overview of Factors that Affect Family Literacy
      Development 14
   The Rationale for Family Literacy Programs 16
   Features of Family Literacy Programs 19
   Evidence for the Success of Family Literacy Programs 20
   Bringing It All Together 26
3. The *Learning Together* Program 29
   Background and Rationale 29
   Timeframe of the *Learning Together* Program 30
   Projected and Intended Objectives of the *Learning
      Together* Program 31
   Curricula Foundation of the *Learning Together* Program .. 31
   Rationale of the *Learning Together* Program 37
4. Method 41
   Pilot Study 41
   Design and Sample 43
   Assessment Instruments: Children 45
   Assessment Instruments: Adults 46
   Interviews 47
   Observations 49
5. Results and Discussion 51
   Quantitative Analyses 51
      Descriptive Data on Children 51
      Descriptive Data on Parents 62
      Effects of Parents' Characteristics on Children's Initial
         Literacy Achievement 69
      Effects of Parents' Characteristics on Their Own CARA
         Graded Passage Score 70
      Effects of Intervention on Children's Literacy Achievement .. 72
      Effects of Intervention on Parents' Literacy Achievement 77

v

  Qualitative Analyses 77
   Results of the Observations 77
   Results of the Interviews 86
  Summary 92

  Post-Program Interviews 92
  Rating of *Learning Together* Program 93
  Effect of Program on Home Literacy Activities 97
  Summary 99

  First Follow-Up Interview 100
  Second Follow-Up Interview 106
  Summary 111

  Third Follow-Up Interview 112
  Summary 114

  Introduction to Families in the Control Group 115
   First Interview 115
   Second Interview 116
   Third Interview (First Year Follow-Up) 117
   Fourth Interview (Second Follow-Up) 119
   Control Group Summary 121

   Similarities Between Treatment and Control Groups 121
   Differences Between Treatment and Control Groups 122

6. Conclusions and Policy Implications 123
  Children's Literacy Development 123
  Parents' Literacy Development 124
  Parents' Ability to Assist 124
  Best Time to Intervene 125
  Parents' Responsivity 125
  Parents' Literacy Experiences 125
  Parents' Observations of Their Children 125
  Concluding Remarks 126

References 127
Index 139

Tables and Figures

Table 3.1 Number of Handouts and Activities for Units 33

Table 3.2 Overview of Creative Play Unit 33

Table 3.3 Overview of Developing Language for Literacy 34

Table 3.4 Overview of Games Unit 34

Table 3.5 Overview of Beginning With Books Unit 35

Table 3.6 Objectives for Beginning With Books Unit 36

Table 3.7 Support from the Literature for Unit Selection 39

Table 5.1 Number of Children by Site, Study Status, and
Sex at Pretest 51

Table 5.2 TERA Alphabet Subtest Means and Standard Deviations
by Study Status and Sex from Pretest to Fourth Follow-Up 52

Table 5.3 TERA Convention Subtest Means and Standard Deviations
by Study Status and Sex from Pretest to Fourth Follow-Up 54

Table 5.4 TERA Meaning Subtest Means and Standard Deviation
by Study Status and SEx from Pretest to Fourth Follow-Up 57

Table 5.5 TERA Total Score Means and Standard Deviations by
Study Status and Sex from Pre-Test to Fourth Follow-Up 58

Table 5.6 Peabody Total Score Means and Standard Deviations by
Study Status and Sex from Pre-Test to Fourth Follow-Up 59

Table 5.7 Number of Parents, Minimum and Maxiumum Scores,
Means and Standard Deviations for CARA Graded Passage
at Each Point in the Study 68

Figure 1 Histograms for the TERA Alphabet Subtest Raw Scores at
Post-Test, 1st Follow-Up, 2nd Follow-Up, and 3rd Follow-up . .55

Figure 2 Histograms for the TERA Convention Subtest Raw Scores
at Pre-Test, Post-Test, 1st Follow-Up, 2nd Follow-Up, and
3rd Follow-Up 56

Figure 3   Histograms for the TERA Meaning Subtest Raw Scores at
            Pre-Test, Post-Test, First Follow-Up, 2nd Follow-Up, and
            3rd Follow-Up 60

Figure 4   Histograms for the TERA Total Raw Scores at Pre-Test,
            Post-Test, 1st Follow-Up, 2nd Follow-Up, and 3rd Follow-Up .61

Figure 5   Histograms for the PPVT Raw Scores at Pre-Test, 1st
            Follow-Up, 2nd Follow-Up, and 3rd Follow-Up 63

Figure 6   Percentage of Parents by Age 64

Figure 7   Percentage of Parents by Ethnicity 64

Figure 8   Percentage of Parents by Number of Children 65

Figure 9   Percentage of Parents by Marital Status 65

Figure 10   Percentage of Parents by Employment Status 66

Figure 11   Percentage of Parents by Highest Grade Completed 66

Figure 12   Percentage of Parents by First Language 67

Figure 13   Percentage of Parents at Each Graded Passage Level 67

Acknowledgments

The authors wish to express their thanks to:

• Parents and families of the children for seeing the value of this study.

• Facilitators and assistants at the host sites for their help and cooperation.

• Maureen Sanders, Executive Director, Sharon Skage, and the staff at the Centre for Family Literacy for their unwavering commitment and cooperation.

• Keith Anderson and Barbara Leung at Alberta Advanced Education, Community Programs.

• Sean Barford, Duane Burton, Jason Daniels, Amanda Dunham, Stephanie Dunsford, Melissa Johnson, Moira Kovats, Shona Lazin, Alyson Letwin, Lingling Ma, Pat Payne, Nabiha Rawdah, Margaret Reine, Heather Sample Gosse, Moira Staples, Debra Wayken, and Roz Zulla for their work on the study ranging from interviews, testing, data coding, data entry, manuscript preparation, and file checks.

• Alexandra Elton, Beth Mackey, and Agnes Maynard warrant special mention. Alexandra was a willing and devoted assistant; Beth was with the study from the outset and her project management is greatly appreciated; and Agnes was our data reliability and coding assistant from the outset.

• Cherie Geering, Paula Kelly, Sharon Kanwal, Josie Nebo, Janet Pearce, and Monda Wadsworth Blanche provided administrative support for the management of this study.

• Randy Randhawa for assistance with the preliminary data analyses.

• Nilambri Ghai, Diana Kaan, Stephanie LaFleur, Lynne Lalonde, and especially Yvette Souque who saw the need for a longitudinal study on family literacy and gave her unqualified support for such a long term study.

• Our funders: the National Literacy Secretariat and the Canadian Language and Literacy Research Network.

About the Authors

Dr. Linda M. Phillips is Professor and Director of the Canadian Centre for Research on Literacy, Killam Annual Professor at the University of Alberta and was the Principal Investigator on this study.

Dr. Ruth Hayden is Professor Emeritus in the Department of Elementary Education at the University of Alberta, President of Alkida International Consulting Ltd, Project Associate at the Canadian Centre for Research on Literacy and was co-investigator on this study.

Dr. Stephen P. Norris is Professor and Canada Research Chair in Scientific Literacy and the Public Understanding of Science, Director, Centre for Research in Youth, Science Teaching and Learning, Department of Educational Policy Studies at the University of Alberta, and was co-investigator on this study.

Chapter One
Introduction

Family literacy is a somewhat new and controversial term in educational research. It has been referred to as a research diaspora (Yaden & Paratore, 2003) because of the lack of consensus on the most fundamental elements such as definitions, participants, practices, measures, and research in the state of knowledge in family literacy (p. 533). Two prior major reviews of family literacy (Purcell-Gates, 2000) and intergenerational literacy within families (Gadsden, 2000) also concluded existing research on family literacy was inadequate. However, they differed on fundamental presuppositions. Purcell-Gates acknowledged the benefits of family literacy programs, whereas Gadsden and others expressed concern that family literacy interventions detrimentally change the ways families interact with their children. Despite the ideological differences in presuppositions and conclusions, each of the two reviews raised fundamentally important concerns. Nonetheless, all would agree far too many children start schooling with lower than desirable language and literacy achievement.

The inequalities of children's cognitive ability are substantial right from the "starting gate" (Lee & Burkam, 2002, p. 1). In a major examination by Lee and Burkam of 16 157 children entering kindergarten in the United States, several startling and revealing conclusions were reported. They include: the average cognitive ability score of children in the high SES group is 60% higher than the scores of the low SES group; race and ethnicity are correlated with SES and 34% of black children and 29% of Hispanic children are in the lowest quintile of SES compared to only 9% of white children; 48% of the families in the lowest SES quintile are single parent families compared to only 10% in the highest quintile; SES as measured by factors such as family educational expectations, access to quality child care, access to a computer, and home reading and television habits were significantly related to children's cognitive skills; and low SES children begin their formal schooling in consistently lower quality schools, which reinforces the inequalities that existed before children reached school age (p. 2, 3). Reducing the inequalities at the starting gate requires that we view family literacy as the most important factor in emergent language and literacy development.

We report on a longitudinal, quasi-experimental, control group study extending across five years of the *Learning Together: Read and Write with Your Child* Program, hereafter referred to as the *Learning Together* program. The program was adapted from the *Family Literacy Demonstration Programmes* carried out in the UK. In addition to standard quantitative measures, we conducted extensive parent interviews on what they want to learn to help themselves and to help their children.

In collaboration with the Centre for Family Literacy, the National Literacy Secretariat, and the Canadian Language and Literacy Research Network (CLLRNet) this five-year longitudinal study was undertaken in the fall of 2001. Data collection for the treatment group began with the pretests of children and their families in September of 2001, posttests in December of 2001, and continued once each year until December 2005. Families from five communities participated.

The main objective of this study was to determine whether beneficial effects accrue from the use of and participation in the *Learning Together* program. Specifically, effects were sought on (1) children's literacy development, (2) parents' literacy development, and (3) parents' ability to assist in the development of their children's literacy. Other objectives included (4) the identification of the time to intervene in children's literacy development for the greatest effect; (5) the documentation of parents' responsivity to opportunities to foster their children's language; (6) reporting what parents say about their own literacy experiences and perceptions prior to, during, and after their participation in the program; and (7) reporting parents' observations about the literacy of their children now in school.

In addition to the comprehensive data collected on the students in the treatment program, performance scores on the same measures were obtained for a random sample of control students and their parents matched on children's age, gender, ethnicity, and SES.

The next chapter provides a review of the relevant research literature on family literacy and intervention programs. The modified *Learning Together* is described in chapter three. The methodology used is the subject of the fourth chapter followed by results and discussion in chapter five. The sixth and final chapter presents conclusions and recommendations.

Chapter Two
Review of Relevant Literature

Almost a century ago, Edmund Burke Huey (1908) wrote in his chapter on learning to read at home, "The secret of it all lies in parents reading aloud to and with the child" (p. 332). Many today endorse and share this widely held belief that family literacy is essential to and necessary for children's acquisition of literacy (Pelletier & Corter, 2005; Phillips & Sample, 2005; Sample Gosse & Phillips, 2006). The rising national and international interest in and attention to parents' involvement in education (Epstein & Connors, 2002), childcare (Kamerman & Kahn, 1997), social and biological development (Keating & Hertzman, 1999), and health (Tinsley, 2003) confirm the benefits of parent involvement in their children's lives. Unfortunately, there is a lack of agreement as to precisely what family literacy is in the research literature and a lack of valid and generalizable conclusions on the success of family literacy intervention programs. The organization of this review focuses first on the question of what family literacy is and provides a brief historical overview of the factors that affect family literacy development. The second section presents research on home literacy experiences and later literacy achievement in order to provide a rationale for family literacy programs. The third section spotlights common features of family literacy programs. The final section calls attention to the evidence for the success of family literacy programs.

What is Family Literacy?

The terms *family* and *literacy* were amalgamated as a concept by Denny Taylor in her well-known ethnographic study published in 1983. In her six-year study, she described the ways families support the literacy development of their children. From the outset, the meaning of the term "family literacy" became subject to multiple interpretations (Anderson, Hiebert, Scott & Wilkinson, 1985; Durkin, 1966; Hess & Holloway, 1984; Sticht & McDonald, 1989; Taylor & Dorsey-Gaines, 1988; Teale &

Sulzby, 1986). Harris and Hodges (1995) defined family literacy in *The Literacy Dictionary* as literacy efforts or activities involving more than one generation (p. 82). They provide a note that a family literacy program generally has three components – literacy for children, literacy for parents, and instruction for adults on how to foster literacy in their children or young adults (p. 82). The International Reading Association (2001) published a brochure, "What is family literacy?" The answer was "getting involved in your child's literacy learning" (p.1). Implicit throughout the brochure was a focus on assisting families in developing literacy skills and gaining an understanding of what is expected of their children once they enter school.

We endorse the view presented by Tracey (1995). She captures many of the important concepts of family literacy: (a) the ways literacy is used within and across families in both mainstream and other cultural settings; (b) the nature of the development, implementation, and evaluation of programs designed to facilitate the literacy growth of family members; and (c) the interconnectedness of literacy use in the home and community and children's future academic achievement in school. In this report, we take family literacy to refer to the second concept of literacy programs for family members. That is, we see the fundamental features of family literacy programs to include a focus on improving the literacy of the children as well as their parents. It is our view that unidimensional programs that focus on just the child's or just the parents' literacy are not effective and that in order to educate children we must also educate their families.

Historical Overview of Factors that Affect Family Literacy Development

The importance of the family as the core environment for the promotion of literacy learning dates back at least 150 years in Canada. Born in 1857, Adelaide Sophia Hunter Hoodless, the first known Canadian Family Educator, made the prescient statement, "A Nation cannot rise above the level of its homes" (British Columbia Women's Institute, 1892). Then, as is the case now, the most pathetic victims of poverty and social ills were women and children. Hoodless is known for her directness, "Educate a boy and you educate a man, but educate a girl and you educate a family" (BCWI, 1892). She saw education as a means of implementing social reform and worked tirelessly to promote the education of families. It can be said that finally family literacy programs have become a topic worthy of discussion in educational settings (Phillips & Sample, 2005, p. 92).

Poverty assuredly is a combination of hunger, unacceptable housing, and few resources but is complicated further by factors such as substance abuse, interpersonal violence, family instability, homelessness, infection, and relatively new syndromes such as fetal alcohol spectrum disorder (FASD). These social risk factors affect the quality of the home environment which in turn negatively affects children's emergent literacy, social competence and language development (Foster, Lambert, Abbott-Shim, McCarty, & Franze, 2005).

Language and literacy development are affected by the home language environment. Studies have shown that the kind of interactions in language use needed for long-term literacy development include opportunities to engage in extended, connected discourse that communicates meaning using varied, precise vocabulary and syntax rather than gesture or reliance on extensive shared knowledge. Children who lack these types of extended discourse do not develop the facility needed to effectively undertake reading and writing tasks (Dickinson & McCabe, 2001). In a document prepared by the National Education Goals Panel, Kagan, Moore, and Bredekamp (1995) examined five dimensions of children's early development and learning: physical well-being and motor development; social and emotional development; approaches to learning including individual, cultural and contextual variation; language development and cognition; and general knowledge. All five dimensions must be considered in a child's learning and development.

Parents need to know and understand how their behavior and lifestyle choices can have immediate effects on their children's lives. For instance, emergent literacy skills are known to provide the foundation to children's success in school. Knowledge of the alphabet at entry into school is one of the strongest single predictors of literacy success in the short and long-term (Adams, 1990; Lonigan, Bloomfield, Anthony, Bacon, Phillips, & Samwel, 1999) and phonological awareness is a key precursor to the acquisition of early reading skills (Wagner & Torgesen, 1987). It comes as no surprise then that there is a strong relation among emergent literacy skills learned at home and future behavior and social competence.

Lonigan, Bloomfield, Anthony, Bacon, Phillips, and Samwel (1999) found that problems of inattention were substantially, consistently, and often uniquely associated with less well developed emergent literacy skills in preschool children (p. 8). Their research and that of others (e.g., Hinshaw, 1992; Shaywitz, Fletcher, & Shaywitz, 1994) has shown that high levels of inattention characteristic of Attention Deficit Hyperactivity Disorder (ADHD) may place children at risk for delays in reading ability. Problems with both inattention and emergent literacy skills place the child at an even greater disadvantage for success in schooling. This disadvantage can be lessened by the ways in which parents interact with their children.

The relationship between specific language impairment in children and parenting behaviors is reciprocal. The amount of speech parents direct to their children affects the child's language development, and, if the child's language development is impaired, then parents sometimes assume greater responsibility in and compensate for the child's conversations (Conti-Ramsden, 1990; Hammer, Tomblin, Zhang, & Weiss, 2001). The consequence is that children with language impairments have fewer opportunities to engage in speech, and have a reduced range in types of conversations resulting in impaired literacy development.

Studies of children from lower income and educational background families have repeatedly shown that they are at a higher risk for reading difficulties (Phillips, Norris & Mason, 1996; Smith & Dixon, 1995); for delays in language development (Lonigan et al., 1999), preschool letter and phonological awareness (Lonigan, Burgess, Anthony, & Barker, 1998), subsequent decoding and comprehension skills (Raz & Bryant, 1990), and cognitive language and literacy development (Dickinson & Tabors, 2001). Thus the language environment in the home, the quality and diversity of the linguistic interactions, and the opportunities for social, behavioral and emotional development through parents reading to and engaging in appropriate learning experiences are critical to children's overall development. Intervention programs aimed at supporting parents in their quest to maximize their children's language and literacy development are advocated extensively.

The Rationale for Family Literacy Programs

The rationale for family literacy programming is based on research suggesting a strong link between home experiences and later literacy achievement. Home environment has been demonstrated to be an important factor in early linguistic and cognitive development. It is also recognized that children are socialized into literacy and that this socialization begins with the family (Heath, 1983; Morrow, 1989; Nickse, 1989; Paratore, 2001; 2002; Purcell-Gates, 2000; Purcell-Gates & Dahl, 1991; Sénéchal, Thomas, & Monker, 1995; Sulzby & Teale, 1991; Taylor, 1983; Teale & Sulzby, 1986).

There is evidence to suggest that children's emergent literacy development is constrained by the ways in which their families use print

(Scarborough, Dobrich & Hager, 1991; Sénéchal, 2006; Sénéchal & LeFevre, 2002). For example, Sénéchal, LeFevre, Thomas, & Daley (1998) have shown that children may be exposed to informal and/or formal literacy experiences at home. In the case of informal literacy experiences, "the goal is the message contained in the print" such as what the story is about. In the formal literacy experiences, the goal is "to focus more on the print per se" such as the identification of particular letters (p. 102). The informal should precede the formal, but both are necessary if children are to acquire literacy. Otherwise, even if children's homes are rich in oral language, they may have difficulty acquiring literacy and may not develop knowledge of written registers. One way to develop such knowledge is through shared book reading. Particular strategies have been identified that can make shared book reading more effective in increasing children's vocabulary and language knowledge (Evans, Shaw, & Bell, 2000). Such strategies include the use of language that takes children beyond the here and now, promotes the development of language skills expected for use in school, and provides experiences that overflow into and make meaningful other areas of life (DeTemple, 2001). Variations in the level and nature of literacy activities in the home account for some of the differences in the ways children understand and produce decontextualized print (Snow, 1983).

Given the preceding points, we know that at least some of the difference in literacy achievement can be explained by variation with print experiences. It is at this point that ideological differences emerge. Questions have been raised about the appropriateness of intervening in the literacy practices of families. Family literacy programs that teach parents mainstream ways of relating to print have been criticized for transmitting the culture of school literacy through the vehicle of the family instead of enhancing the family's home literacy (Auerbach, 1989). Concerns have been raised that some family literacy programs are predicated on deficiencies in family literacy practices and attitudes (Auerbach, 1995a, 1995b). There are those who assert that family literacy interventions imply that families bear primary responsibility for any literacy, economic, and educational problems they may face. The fear is that this implication will divert attention away from social and political factors that may play an even greater role (Auerbach, 1995a, 1995b; Taylor & Dorsey-Gaines, 1988).

Advocates of family literacy programs, however, endorse strongly the positive benefits of intervention, particularly for lower-income families headed by parents with low levels of literacy. This endorsement is supported by research showing that it is difficult for these parents to support, as much as they might like, their children's literacy development and to pass on positive attitudes about schooling and the importance of learning to read and write (Newman & Beverstock, 1990; Paratore, 2001; Saracho & Spodek, 2005). Family literacy researchers have noted also that many of these parents want to know how to help their children with literacy and resent not being taught specific strategies for reading with their children (Edwards, 1991, 1995; McKeough, Phillips, Timmons, & Lupart, 2006; Phillips & Sample, 2005; Sample Gosse & Phillips, 2006). Supporters of family literacy programs strive to demonstrate that interventions can meet a need that the families themselves recognize and can do so in ways that are respectful of their cultural and personal values.

In addition to questions about the appropriateness of intervening in the literacy practices of families, there are questions of whether there is any place for teaching literacy in preschool. In Britain, and many other countries in the 1970s and 1980s, for example, there was a reluctance to acquiesce to the pressures from parents and teachers to "start children off early in reading and writing." The extent of the resistance was evident in the fact that alternatives were emphasized, "pictures not words, paint brushes not pens, pictures of animals, flowers or toys in place of children's names in the cloakroom" (Hannon, 1995, p. 55). This avoidance of literacy by preschool teachers was in response to the use of quite inappropriate methods at an early age. These included having the children sit for extended periods of time for rote learning, drill and practice; a heavy emphasis on perceptual skills; and flashcard activities. By the 1990s matters started to change and there was a shift away from a school-centred view of preschool literacy.

Her Majesty's Inspectors conducted a review of the education of children less than five years of age (HMI, 1989). They concluded that preschool children saw lots of environmental print, they wanted to read, and that some children already were reading. Concurrently, the National Curriculum was introduced and it spelled out the targets of attainment for children from ages 5 to 16 years of age (DES, 1989). The targets at five years interestingly were designed on a strong emergent literacy base. The implication was that preschools were expected to engage in literacy practices and to prepare children for a smooth transition into schools. Even though some preschool teachers preferred that parents not "get involved," many parents were actively promoting their children's literacy development (Hannon & James, 1990, p. 62).

There have been many studies of home-focused involvement in emergent literacy. Some national and international examples include those in Canada (Hayden & Phillips, 2000; Phillips, Norris & Mason, 1996), in

Britain (Griffiths & Edmonds, 1986; Wade, 1984; Swinson, 1985); in Israel (Levin, Patel, Margalit, & Barad, 2002; Ravid & Tolchinksky, 2002); in the Netherlands (see Bus, van Ijzendoorn & Pellegrini, 1995 for a meta-analysis); and in the United States (Edwards, 1989; Locke, 1986; McCormick & Mason, 1986; Segel & Friedberg, 1991; Winter & Rouse, 1990). These home-focused intergenerational initiatives showed considerable potential for the engagement of parents in their children's emergent literacy development. The implications for policy, practice and research are many: greater collaboration between preschools, homes and schools is needed; and an acceptance that there is significant variation in children's language and literacy experiences, that some children's literacy may be different than that expected by the schools, and that there is a critical need for experimental longitudinal studies. Implicit in this discussion about children's literacy at home is the role of the parents. As Peter Hannon (1995) so elegantly said, "the family – (is) the social group in which the parents' and the children's literacies meet, within which they use literacy, develop their literacy, and interact in literacy activities" (p. 103). Programs aimed to improve the parents' literacy as well as the child's are the subjects of the next section.

Features of Family Literacy Programs

Family literacy programs share common features. According to Neuman (1998), family literacy programs offer literacy instruction to members of families, involve participants in curriculum planning and development, create supportive learning environments, provide opportunities for the formation of family and social networks, and actively collaborate with other social and educational services.

Family literacy programs that incorporate early childhood programming and adult education along with an element of parents and children working together have been referred to as comprehensive programs (Wasik, Dobbins, & Herrmann, 2001). These programs presume that the skills learned and practiced by the adult and the child produce an intergenerational and/or reciprocal transfer of skills (Neuman, 1998) that can vary in the relative emphasis on the child and adult components (Hendrix, 1999). Within the child-focused component, developmentally appropriate experiences are offered to promote language and literacy learning. The experiences are designed not only to impart skills but also to encourage a positive attitude towards learning. The adult literacy instruction is typically geared to the goals of the individuals, either relating to parent-child learning or to employment (Brizius & Foster, 1993). The joint parent-child activities are focused on families learning how to become a greater part of the world of print and are designed to promote interactions that lead to greater understanding, communication, and skills.

Facilitators promote parents' awareness of their own knowledge and capabilities for helping their children (Rodriguez-Brown & Meehan, 1998). They also provide opportunities for lower-income parents and children to learn and practice strategies demonstrated to be successful for middle-income parents and children. In these cases, family literacy facilitators serve as coaches for participating families as they acquire new skills, which may include techniques for book sharing, questioning, language facilitation, and providing positive feedback to children (Wasik et al., 2001). Many programs also specifically seek to provide opportunities for parents to support parents, provide time for sharing of experiences, and discuss ways to overcome obstacles to family learning.

Family literacy advocates have recognized the need to develop a range of models that respond to different family structures and build on the strengths and history of each cultural group. Where different program models are not feasible, program providers are urged to be sensitive to cultural differences and to build on the diversity of the participants and the assets of each cultural group (Brizius & Foster, 1993). Programs have also been tailored to the needs of families through collaboration with education, social service, health, and employment programs. Family literacy programs also typically provide support services such as transportation, childcare, and appropriate scheduling for participants.

Evidence for the Success of Family Literacy Programs

Family literacy programs are diverse. It is not our intention to canvas the evaluations of all programs in use but rather to examine those that are widely discussed and endorsed. There has been a dearth of studies on the efficacy of family literacy programs within high quality research parameters. Well known programs such as *Head Start* and *Even Start* have a clear and unequivocal focus on "the needs of young children" and not on those of the adults. In the case of *Head Start*, the conclusion reached by Mills (1998) that it is "arguably the best investment America has ever made in its youngest citizens" (p. 2) provides further evidence that the child is the primary focus and work with parents is primarily to support the children's development (Edmiaston & Fitzgerald, 2003, p. 175).

Even Start includes four components: parent literacy education, child literacy education, child activity time, and parenting education. The goal is "to help break the cycle of poverty and illiteracy by improving the educational opportunities available to low-income families with limited educational experiences" (St. Pierre, Gamse, Alamprese, Rimdzius, & Tao, 1998). Paratore (2002) explores the practice of the *Even Start* family literacy program and summarizes its effectiveness. She makes a number of telling points, including: (a) with the exception of one small-scale study, there is no control group to verify that gains are attributable to *Even Start* participation; (b) on measures used to assess changes in parenting behaviors, employment status, and income all increased but neither of these indicators was greater than those for control families (p. 14); and (c) the data on the importance of parenting education were conflicting, sometimes showing a positive relationship and sometimes no relationship.

The evaluation conducted by the National Foundation for Educational Research (NFER) for the British Skills Agency (BSA) Family Literacy Demonstration Programs in the United Kingdom and entitled *Family Literacy Works* (Brooks, Gorman, Harman, Hutchison, & Wilkin, 1996) claimed just that – family literacy works. It was characterized as a comprehensive approach to family literacy. We have gone into detail on this study because it is the one on which Alberta Learning and the National Literacy Secretariat decided to support a *Learning Together* Program in Alberta. The authors of the *Family Literacy Works* report examined four pilot family literacy demonstration programs in multiple-deprivation areas of Cardiff, Liverpool, Norfolk, and North Tyneside. The program had two goals: "to raise standards of literacy among adults . . . and their children, and to extend awareness of the importance of literacy and the role of the family" (p. 4). The programs lasted 96 hours over 12 weeks; were provided for children ages 3 to 6 years and their parents; and had three components (parents' literacy, children's literacy, and joint sessions for the children and parents). The principal judgments and recommendations of the evaluation were that the programs "achieved great success." The Basic Skills Agency's Family Literacy Demonstration Programmes was judged to be "one of the most effective they had ever encountered, and well worth building on," and the Family Literacy initiative should therefore "be continued and made available more widely across the country" (p. xv).

What was the evidence for these claims that family literacy works? The evaluation collected quantitative and qualitative data on both the parents and children. Quantitative data for the first two cohorts of families (Summer 1994; Autumn 1994) were collected at the beginning and ending of the program, at 12 weeks, and 9 month follow-ups. For the third cohort of families (Spring 1995), data were collected at the beginning, ending, and 12 week follow-up. For the fourth cohort of families (Summer 1995) data were collected only at the beginning and ending of the program. Qualitative data included interviews with parents towards the end of each course/program and on each follow-up occasion. Interviews with coordinators and facilitators took place each term and teachers' impressions were gathered in the spring and summer of 1995 only.

Parents' literacy was estimated through the use of a three-part reading cloze test; a three-part informal writing task which was assessed impressionistically; and a 35 item six-point scale on home literacy activities. Assessment of children's (beyond 4 years of age) vocabulary and literacy development included three parts: writing which ranged from a drawing to a few lines depending on what the child could do; and the *Peabody Picture Vocabulary Test (PPVT) – Revised Form L* used to assess vocabulary and the reading recognition subtest of the *Peabody Individual Achievement Tests (PIAT)* used to assess reading. *The Family Literacy Works Study,* that is the NFER Evaluation study (Brooks, Gorman, Harman, Hutchison, & Wilkin, 1996) was neither an experimental nor a quasi-experimental study and children less than four years of age were not tested using the PPVT even though it is designed for persons 2½ years. No control sample of either children or parents existed for this study. The adult cohorts at the start of and across the four pilot programs in the summer of 1994, autumn 1994, spring 1995 and summer 1995 were 86, 103, 102, and 88 respectively. They report that by the end of the 9 month follow-up the numbers of adults had dropped to 34 and 54 but without clarification we cannot know what this means because it appears they are comparing two groups to four. There were no follow-ups for spring and summer 1995. The child cohorts at the start of and across the four pilot programs in the summer of 1994, autumn 1994, spring 1995 and summer 1995 were 77, 106, 112, and 97. Again, they report that by the end of the 9 month follow-up, the numbers of children had dropped to 59 and 66 and the comparison is two groups to four. No follow-ups for spring and summer 1995 were reported.

Some further concerns about the *Family Literacy Works Study* in addition to the fact that it was not a matched control group design include, that the younger children were not administered standardized measures, that parents' reading was assessed on a right only answer on a non-standardized cloze test. It is widely known that the cloze was developed in 1953 as a tool to measure readability and that it cannot be considered a valid measure of authentic reading ability. In the final analysis, the study was neither longitudinal nor experimental and while the reported results are encouraging, the claim that family literacy works remains to be demonstrated. No conclusion can be drawn that gains can be attributed to program effects.

Much of the information used to justify family literacy interventions initially came from research into individual program components and from positive anecdotal reports. For example, the children's component of family literacy programs was most often defended in terms of the success of other initiatives that promoted early childhood development. Adult programming was likewise connected to research into the benefits of adult education. Synergistic effects of parents and children learning together were often assumed or bolstered by anecdotal reports.

In 1991 the National Center for Family Literacy (NCFL) in the United States published a summary of the positive outcomes of family literacy programs. The Center concluded that the initiatives increased the developmental skills of preschool children and the parenting skills and educational levels of participating parents. Positive effects on the parent-child relationships were documented. Parents were described as becoming familiar with and comfortable in the school setting and as providing a role model for the child by showing interest in education. While the NCFL study provided some indications of the success of family literacy programs, it was acknowledged that additional research was needed (Brizius & Foster, 1993).

Moreover, concerns have been raised about whether many of the so-called family literacy programs are indeed concerned with family literacy or with political and economic interests. In some programs there is a lack of focus on family literacy (Hannon, 1995) resulting from a theoretical vacuum because the adult basic education (ABE) tradition and the early childhood education (ECE) have not truly merged. There is a greater emphasis on the interactions with children. Consequently, parents' literacy development is neglected. Finally, there is the matter for which families a literacy program is appropriate. Children from families with low income coupled with low literacy abilities have a 72 percent chance of being in the lowest reading level, compared to 25 percent for children as a whole (ALBSU, 1993). This finding does not mean, however, that only these children are the ones who will benefit the most from a program. Unfortunately, it may be an uphill struggle to persuade parents to get literacy education for themselves even though they are prepared to attend programs to help their children. For example, Bynner and Fogelman (1993) found that "less than one-fifth of those who reported literacy problems had attended an adult literacy class" (p. 57).

The patterns of participation in Canadian literacy and upgrading programs convinced Long and Middleton, (2001) that recruitment and retention are a significant challenge within the literacy field. Of those people who contact a literacy group, fewer than half actually enroll and of those who enroll thirty percent drop out. The bottom line is that only thirty-five percent of eligible Canadians participated in literacy and upgrading programs. The most recent education indicators in Canada (Canadian Education Statistics Council, 2006) reported that four out of ten adult Albertans do not have the requisite literacy skills to function well in today's world. Of that group, 14 percent are at level 1, the lowest level of literacy attainment, which means they are unable to read their children a bedtime story. A further 26% are at level 2, defined as ability to read simple and clearly laid out text. The indicators reported also that for Canadians generally, the lowest levels of participation in adult education and training occurred among those with a secondary school graduation or less. These results are juxtaposed with the fact that in 2001 "no other OECD nation had a higher proportion of its population aged 25 to 64 with either a college or university credential than Canada. However, in terms of the population with a university degree, Canada ranked fifth overall" (p. xvi). The upshot is that there are many adults who are candidates for engagement in family literacy programs designed to improve both the literacy level of the adults and their children.

It is not our intention to canvas the different theoretical assumptions around family literacy. Challenges of how to best measure the effects of family literacy programs have been raised (Delgato-Gaitan, 1996; Paratore, 2001) on the grounds of the lack of congruence between the ways families use literacy to negotiate the daily activities of their lives and the ways literacy is assessed in schools (Taylor & Strickland, 1989), of how to find out in valid and reliable ways what *really* goes on in homes (Purcell-Gates, 1993), and of the appropriation of cultural practice (Serpell, 1997). We acknowledge that these are important and complex issues. At best, we can ensure that in our research we have used some of the best instruments available for the purposeful collection of data on children and on adults (IRA, 1999).

Despite an ongoing call for additional investigations into the efficacy of family literacy, research has continued to lag behind practice. This lag is troubling because of the critical role the evaluation process should play in informing practice. Family literacy providers need to be able to identify what, if any, difference their programs make in the lives of participants and in their community. They also have a need to assess individual progress of the parent and child participants and factors affecting that progress. The effectiveness of each component of family literacy must be ascertained along with possible interactive and reciprocal effects of combinations of components. All of this information is useful in determining ways to improve family literacy programs so that they better serve participating families. Demonstrating the value of family literacy programs through research is also necessary to compete effectively for resources.

Several difficulties in conducting literacy research with very young children and with parents of low educational levels are acknowledged. One is that reliable and valid literacy measurement at ages 2½ to 5 years is difficult to obtain because it is a time when children's understanding of literacy is still emerging, and their progress is uneven (Phillips, Norris, & Mason, 1996). A second difficulty is that many parents with low levels of education have less than positive attitudes about schooling and literacy activities and may choose not to participate in programs if required to participate in evaluations of their reading. These barriers are not insurmountable. Outcomes for participating children can be determined by using multiple measures of their vocabulary and early reading development. Parents may be less reluctant to participate in program evaluation if they are met on their own terms and care is taken to use non-threatening methods of data collection (Phillips & Sample, 2006).

Family literacy programs which usually target low income and low literacy level families have been investigated for over three decades. It is known and widely accepted that children's literacy begins long before they start school and that their preschool experiences play a critical role in their school achievement. These preschool experiences differ depending on parents' level of education and home literacy practices which are often embedded in their daily routines. It is less widely accepted that children fail not because their language and literacy are deprived but rather because they are different from that expected at schools. All agree that it is important to bridge the gap between the literacy of the home and that of the school and that studies with methodological rigor are needed to provide the much-needed evidence of how best to serve those families.

Family literacy has been studied from a diverse set of methodological approaches including case studies (Whitehead, 2002), ethnography (Heath, 1983), observation (Teale, 1986), interviewing (Weinberger, 1996), and randomized control (Nutbrown et al., 2005). A study of parents' experiences of a family literacy program in a northern city in England revealed that parents felt the program had benefited the children and that it may have had an impact on their family literacy practices generally (Hannon, Morgan, & Nutbrown, 2006). Taken together these and other studies have expanded our understanding of family literacy and informed our perceptions of how to conceive of the literacy practices within families.

On February 14, 2006, Tom Sticht, an international consultant in adult education, proposed a life cycles education policy perspective in order to stop functional illiteracy at its sources. He referred to the National Assessment of Adult Literacy (NAAL) published in 2005 that reported one in six, that is 30 000 000 adult Americans are functionally illiterate and that for 13 and 17 year olds, their reading achievement increases as their parents' level of education increases. The research of Morrison, Bachman and Connor (2005) on improving literacy in America questioned preschool programs that do not focus on improving parenting skills, "preschool programs without parent outreach and adult education are not effective" (pp, 48, 49). Torres (2003) argued that "Adult Basic Education and Learning (ABLE) cannot continue to be viewed in isolation, as a separate educational goal . . . to educate children, it is essential to educate adults" (p. 4). The Life Cycles policy that Sticht refers to is one that calls governments to invest in adult literacy and lifelong education with the "understanding that this investment will not only provide returns in terms of increased productivity, health, and civic participation on the part of adults, but also with the understanding that the investment in the education of adults may also produce returns in the increased educability of their children" (p. 4).

The economic, fiscal, and social benefits of investment in early childhood development (ECD) report exceptional returns. A study by Lynch (2004) provides the investment costings and dividends for high quality ECD programs including adult education programs that consistently generate cost ratios exceeding 3 to 1. He goes on to say, "Within 25 years, if a nationwide program were started, the budget benefits would exceed costs by $31 billion" (p. 2). Based on a population of approximately one-tenth of that of the United States, the prorated budget benefits for Canada if it invested in ECD would be $3.1 billion, assuming all other factors are more or less equal.

Bringing It All Together

We acknowledge that families are looking for ways "to support transition between home and school" (Rodriquez-Brown, 2003) as they plan for the future of their children. The families in our *Learning Together* program declare that there is a "book world" beyond their everyday local literacies and they want it for their children (Phillips & Sample Gosse, 2005). Much has been written about the importance of breaking with everyday experience in order to see the range of options for living and thinking beyond the here and now (Floden & Buchmann, 1993). All families live at a particular time and in a particular place, "but school and university are places apart where a declared learner is emancipated from the limitations of his local circumstances and from the wants he may have acquired, and is moved by intimations of what he has never yet dreamed" (Oakeshott, 1989, p. 24). Perhaps without even knowing anything of Oakeshott's views, all families want their children to be successful in school for reasons similar to those of John Dewey (1916/1966): it is "the office of the school environment . . . to see to it that each individual gets an opportunity to escape from the limitations of the social group in which he was born, and to come into living contact with a broader environment" (p. 20) and to have choices.

We have seen parents in our research from very different cultures, yet they long to enjoy what Shirley Brice Heath (1991) calls "the sense of being literate" and they are dedicated to ensuring that their children are able to partake in a world beyond the here and now. These parents understand that the sense of being literate provides an important challenge to firsthand experience which "limits not only personal understandings but views of the social and political worlds" (Buchmann & Schwille, 1993, p. 26). They want to use their local literacies to engage in the more formal literacies of schooling. Breaks with everyday experience are necessary for all children to think and act with a sense of methods and ideas that reach beyond the immediately given. However, these breaks come at a cost. As Floden and Buchmann (1993) state, "Equalizing opportunities often disconnect individuals from their backgrounds" (p. 48) and increase the distance from that which is deeply personal and cherished. To live is to learn and to learn means to alter, and in so doing the familiar is changed, as are the interactions between and among families and their children. We see that when the families' own perspectives are taken into account, the gains they perceive justify the opening up of alternative interactions for those who choose to participate in family literacy programs.

To return to the beginning of our chapter, we judge the conclusion by Yaden and Paratore, "family literacy is a research diaspora" to be an overstatement. Indeed, there are a number of mistaken assumptions by many educators, social workers, and politicians that family literacy programs will solve educational and social ills despite issues of race, poverty, and gender. Some mistaken assumptions include pervasive beliefs that there is an absence of literacy practices, a lack of interest in their children, and bad parenting in the homes of the poor and uneducated. Programs built on assumptions that imply families are responsible for their educational and economic circumstances would undoubtedly lead to questionable results. Those who work with families as they struggle for a life of dignity for their children and then for themselves know the fallacy of these assumptions.

We have found large funds of knowledge in families, families who care deeply and profoundly about their children, and families who hold beliefs about how best to help their children be successful in school. We corroborate the work of Yberra (1999) on Latino life in the United States: "Despite our diversity, we are nonetheless bound by a common search for a better life for ourselves and our children" (p. 84). In accord with the work of Sénéchal et al. (1998), the families in our study (Phillips & Sample, 2005) expressed a desire to learn more about the ways to engage in formal literacy experiences wherein the goal is to focus more on the print so that their children would be better prepared to understand and engage in what Catherine Snow (1983) calls decontextualized print and Shirley Brice Heath (1991) calls the sense of being literate.

We agree with Yaden and Paratore (2002) that literacy is a complex phenomenon. Answers about the efficacy of family literacy programs cannot be obtained through research unless we know what questions to ask.

Chapter Three
The Learning Together Program

Background and Rationale

Based on the report, "Family Literacy Works," of a Basic Skills Agency (BSA) Demonstration Family Literacy Programme (Brooks, Gorman, Harman, Hutchison, & Wilkin, 1996), the Alberta Advanced Education and Career Development Department created the Intensive Family Literacy Initiative Fund in early 1999 (Prospects Literacy Association, 2000, p. 3). The aim was to fund a program to meet the literacy needs of families in Alberta. A replication of the Basic Skills Agency Program was co-ordinated by The Centre for Family Literacy Project at Prospects Literacy Association (PLA) in Edmonton. Funds for the developmental stage of this program were requested from the National Literacy Secretariat of Human Resources Development Canada specifically for a four-month initial project to lay the groundwork for this model. The project had three stages: (1) an initial development phase, (2) delivery of a pilot model, and (3) a revision of this model and the delivery of subsequent programs.

In the initial development phase, two committees were created: the Adaptation Committee and the Advisory Committee (PLA, 2000, p. 3). The former was responsible for examining the BSA Program and reporting any revisions needed for an adaptation of the program in Alberta. The Advisory Committee was created to provide direction to the initiative and ensure there was continuity between the project and other related initiatives. Throughout this time, meetings were held to discuss the evaluation of the UK programs and to provide detailed feedback to the Canadian program developers.

The pilot study began in September 1999 and ended in April 2000 (Hayden & Phillips, 2000) (PLA, 2000, p. 4). The aims of this phase were to continue the delivery of the pilot programs for the first three months of 2000, make any necessary changes to the pilot program and create research possibilities and evaluation tools for longitudinal research and offer future programs using the modified program based on the pilot. A companion proposal from a research team at the University of Alberta was developed to examine the success of the program including areas such as the adaptation of the curriculum and the materials and participant satisfaction (Hayden & Phillips, 2000) (PLA, 2000, p.4). Recommendations were made to the program before the launch of Phase Two and a grant proposal was developed to implement the longitudinal research.

The pilot programs were offered over a three month period totalling 90 hours and comprised of three integrated components: adult learning, preschool education and parent-child joint sessions. Two sites for the delivery of the pilot programs included an urban and a rural setting and the target groups were families with parents with low education and income and preschool children who were at risk of not succeeding in school. The possibility to accredit adult sessions and use the Manitoba Certificate in Literacy and Learning as a curriculum was discussed in meetings.

The goals of the study were to deliver the revised family literacy pilot program and to start the evaluation of the program. Funding for this came from the province through the Community Programs at Alberta Learning. In March 2000, a proposal was submitted to cover costs such as the revision made based on the pilot program and co-ordination of the programs in two communities (PLA, 2000, p. 4).

Timeframe of the *Learning Together* Program

The program was delivered over a three month period, three mornings or afternoons per week totalling 90 hours. The first two sessions involved separate adult and early-years group sessions with each group having its own facilitator. In the last session each day, parents paired up with their child for a 30-minute session to practice newly acquired skills and knowledge while two facilitators remained in the room to oversee the sessions.

Projected and Intended Objectives of the *Learning Together* Program

The *Learning Together* program aimed to improve the child's literacy, parents' literacy, and strengthen the ability of the parents to develop their child's literacy. Short-term goals for this project included an increase in the emergent literacy skills of preschool age participants, increase the use of home literacy activities by participants, and accredit parents within the adult curriculum (PLA, 2000, p. 5). Long-term goals involved the improvement of literacy rates for adult and children participants including an increase in parental participation in children's education, increase communication between parent and child and, increase success for children at school and increased participation in further learning by parents.

Curricula Foundation of the *Learning Together* Program

Detailed curriculum information on the BSA program model was unavailable although the book, *Family Literacy Works* (Brooks et al., 1996) provides an outline, labeled "descriptions of the family literacy demonstration programmes" (p. 8-11). It should be noted that the term "curriculum" has a different meaning in the United Kingdom where a list of topics on a single page may suffice whereas in Canada the term has the connotation of a total program with objectives, resources, and activities to be included in addition to the themes to be explored.

In order to meet the somewhat more prescriptive demands of the Canadian educational system, the coordinator of the *Learning Together* program, in collaboration with colleagues and specialists in the fields of adult, early literacy development, and childhood education developed a comprehensive curriculum for use in the program. The Alberta curriculum is directly related to the BSA curriculum and built upon other BSA documents (e.g. *Preparing for Early Literacy Education with Parents* developed by Nutbrown and Hannon (1997), and two Canadian publications, *Families at School: A Guide for Educators* (Thomas, Fazio, & Stiefelmeyer, 1999a), and *Families at School: A Guide for Parents* (Thomas, Fazio, & Stiefelmeyer, 1999b).

The curriculum for the *Learning Together* program includes eight key units for each adult component, early-years component, and joint sessions component. It provides considerable detail for what each component might include and a range of appropriate activities/resources that program facilitators might use within a unit. The themes for each unit are:

32 *Family Literacy Matters*

Creative Play

Developing Language for Literacy

Games

Beginning with Books

Early Reading

Writing and Drawing

Environmental Print

Advice and Guidance

These themes mirrored to a considerable degree those offered in the BSA programs. The units were not intended to be used as weekly plans, some were longer than others and required more than one week to complete, conversely other units required less time. Furthermore, activities in each of the units presented in the curriculum were coordinated across the adult-only, early-years-only, and joint session components of the program. It is also important to note that facilitators were advised to respect and build on parents' existing skills and abilities within each of the units and to capitalize upon their knowledge whenever possible. In addition, the curriculum was not designed as a step-by-step prescription for the delivery of the program. As facilitators had been hired based on their expertise and knowledge in their respective areas, considerable flexibility was expected of them in how they approached and worked through the units. Each unit was accompanied by a selection of activities, and in the case of the adult-only sessions, a selection of handouts from which facilitators could choose to use as they saw fit.

Each of the units had a list of suggested activities, designed to reinforce and expand upon the theme under review. These activities were also supported by handouts for parental use which the participants kept in binders. Some handouts contained templates for parental use and others were short readings that related to the theme under discussion. In Table 3.1, the number of suggested activities and handouts are identified.

Tables 3.2 – 3.5 demonstrate how four units were coordinated across the three components of the program. The tables deal with creative play, language, games, and books.

Table 3.6 provides the objectives for the unit on beginning with books.

Table 3.1
Number of Handouts and Activities for Units

Unit	Activities	Handouts
Creative Play	10	2
Developing Language and Literacy	10	5
Games	7	2
Beginning with Books	11	8
Early Reading	12	9
Writing and Drawings	15	10
Environmental Print	7	2
Advice and Guidance	0	0

Table 3.2
Overview of Creative Play Unit

Adult Component	Early Years Component	Child /Adult Joint Session
Importance of children's play	Play games, play alone / in centres	
Relationship of play to literacy		Participate in play
Relationship of play to learning		
	Create centres to foster play	Observe play
Use of praise	Extend story reading to extend play activities	
Parents as partners in play activities	Use props (e.g., masks, hats) to foster imaginative play	Follow child choice for play activities

Table 3.3
Overview of Developing Language for Literacy

Adult Component	Early Years Component	Child / Adult Joint Session
Importance of rhymes and songs	Songs, nursery rhymes, finger plays	Using rhymes / songs
Opportunities to use imagination		
Use of toys /role play to stimulate language	Use of print in centres	Making puppets
Use of puppetry and finger plays	Role play with props	Participating in centres
Family storytelling	Wordless books	
Parents as models for language growth	Games with texture	Making craft from story
Relationship of speaking / listening to literacy	Developing speaking and listening abilities	

Table 3.4
Overview of Games Unit

Adult Component	Early Years Component	Child / Adult Joint Session
Relationship of games to literacy development	Playing games	Sharing games made by parents
	Gross motor and fine motor games	
Playing games as a family activity	Playing together	Extending language / print through games
Different types of games	Playing traditional games	
Making games		

Table 3.5
Overview of Beginning With Books Unit

Adult Component	Early Years Component	Child / Adult Joint Session
Personal memories of book sharing	Library play centre	Library tour
Discussion on when to start reading to children	Bookstore play centre	Library membership
What do your children know about stories	Make signs to sort books	Sharing books made
Jigsaw of development with books	Make library cards	
Examine a range of different books	Make individual books	
Techniques for sharing books	Examine different books pop-up, concept, etc.	
Planning tour of library	Reread favorite books	

Facilitators explained the objectives of each unit to parents and provided supplementary reading materials to support the content of the unit. These materials were brief and written at an easy-to-read level. Facilitators also collected current newspaper and magazine articles on topics related to the units and provided copies as extra reading material for the parents. In addition, facilitators provided opportunities in each session for the parents to have a hands-on experience practicing an activity that they could use with their children in the joint sessions or at home.

During the pilot stage of the *Learning Together* program, the adult sessions included the option for parents to work on one of the three stages in the "Certificate in Literacy and Learning" which had been borrowed with permission from Manitoba Education and Training. The intention was that this certificate could be used in the same way the *WordPower* program was used in the BSA demonstration programs. Unfortunately, there were many problems with the certificate, some of which included that it is not recognized within the Alberta educational system, that it took longer time than the *Learning Together* program allowed for completion, and did not appeal to the parents in the program. Hence, the certificate route was abandoned but not the program for adults. Facilitators wove adult literacy aspects such as spelling, grammar, punctuation, reading comprehension, reading fluency, library skills, etc., into their daily practice, and consistently modeled these skills during their daily interactions with parents.

Table 3.6
Objectives for Beginning With Books Unit

Adult Component	Early Years Component	Child / Adult Joint Session
Discuss how sharing books can have lasting benefits	Develop listening skills	Promote communication between parent and child
Discover range of books and tapes	Contribute to stories by predicting, retelling, etc.	
Join library if desired	Share books with parents	Encourage enjoyment between dyads
Learn about opportunities for learning and for fun to be had with books	Take care of books	
Practice activities to be used in joint sessions and at home	Identify favorite books	Experience library as occasion for family outing
Make book for child		

Within the early-years units, facilitators provided a predictable pattern to the session, regardless of the content of the unit. Children got to know the "rhythm of the day" by moving from free play, to circle time, to snack time, to story time, to directed activities, and to the joint interaction time with their parents. Within that familiar pattern, the children learned to know what to expect and when it would occur. The joint sessions were designed so that parents could practice the new skills and knowledge they gained in the adult sessions on child development. Parents applied their skills and knowledge in planning and implementing the joint sessions with their children. As the program progressed, parents were encouraged to take greater responsibility for guiding and supporting their children's development and in deciding how joint sessions might evolve.

Rationale of the *Learning Together* Program

The field of family literacy has blossomed considerably over the past three decades. Gone are the days when families were warned about teaching their children to read and write. Rather, the academic and professional perspectives today maintain that children are lured into literacy and become knowledgeable about print during their preschool years as a result of the variety of print representations they see manifested within the routines of family and community life. How the children are attracted to literacy learning is primarily dependent on the relationships between them and the significant readers in their lives. The *Learning Together* program is built upon this premise: parental interactive strategies, and the quantity and variety of print materials available in the home are factors that affect children's preparation for meaningful formal literacy instruction.

Although there have been concerns within the literature that family literacy programs mirror mainstream or school-based literacy practices (Whitehouse & Colvin, 2001), promote deficit notions for immigrant or working class families by ignoring the socio-cultural contexts of literacy events within these families (Auerbach,1995a1995b), or advocate for storybook reading as the primary literacy event for leading children into literacy (Anderson, Anderson, Lynch & Shapiro, 2003), the *Learning Together* program was designed upon a "strengths-based" model. This model incorporates the life experiences of individuals as integral to program design and implementation and accepts that the socio-cultural contexts of participants be recognized and valued. Furthermore, rather than "fixing" families to meet mainstream standards, the *Learning Together* program seeks to incorporate and extend what participant families currently do as launch pads for weaving literacy more intentionally into family routines.

Parents of low income and with low education with preschool children considered at risk for future school failure were our focus. Our focus on this group of families was deliberate because it is known their children are much less likely at kindergarten entry to recognize the letters of the alphabet, write their own names, be familiar with book knowledge, and have a sophisticated vocabulary compared to that of their more financially secure and better educated family peers (Lee & Burkham, 2002; Neumann, 2005). It is the conventional wisdom for those in the area of early and family literacy that early intervention programs need to provide parents with the ways and means to provide intentional support for oral language and literacy development.

While it must be recognized that less fortunate parents want to do the best for their children, circumstances of poverty and low education may thwart their efforts to do so. For example, access to the public library may not be possible because of transportation difficulties, inability to pay for library subscriptions or late fines or the lack of knowledge that wide selections of children's books are available. Moreover, those who live in poorer areas of a community may not even have a public library or have one that has extremely limited hours of operation. In short, as this one example demonstrates, parental desire to assist children's development may be eroded by several obstacles beyond their control. Poverty and low education frequently contribute to the lack of stimulating experiences and print materials in the home and especially so if coupled with parental inability to provide an emotionally supportive learning environment. Neuman (2005) maintains there is a "knowledge gap" with respect to low income children's beginning experiences with print as a result of the financial difficulties faced by their families. Furthermore, unless intervention programs offer rich literacy experiences for these children and their families, this knowledge gap will continue to exist even after children enroll in formal schooling.

Recognizing the many impediments faced by at-risk parents who wish to assist their children to move into formal education with a greater chance of success than they themselves experienced, the *Learning Together* program was designed to maximize parental involvement in children's development within a support framework that was realistic, pragmatic and practical. In other words, developing and implementing a curriculum that emphasized oral language and literacy activities that parents could put into practice with comparative ease and that demanded little or no financial burden became the cornerstone for developing the themes around which the adult only, child only, and joint parent-child sessions were organized. In addition, by discussing reading and writing about their children's growth into literacy, parents' own literacy abilities would be enriched and lead to greater involvement with print for their own and their children's needs. Furthermore, the objectives of the themes (units) incorporated the importance of certain features inherent in intervention programming as indicated by the research. Table 3.7 provides a thumbnail sketch of the wealth of literature that supports such themes as core components of an early intervention program.

Table 3.7
Support From the Literature for Unit Selection

Unit	Research
Creative Play	Christie (1991); Gregory (2001); Pelligrini & Galda (1991)
Developing Language for Literacy	Heath (1983); Whitehead (1999)
Games	Brown (1984); Stainthorp & Hughes (2000)
Beginning with Books	Doake (1988); Sulzby (1991)
Early Reading	Goodman (1984, 1986); Scarborough & Dobrich (1994)
Writing and Drawing	Dyson (1989); Kendrick (2003)
Day Out (Environment Print)	Hill (1989); Neumann & Roskos (1993)

In developing the content of the curriculum, efforts were made to make it sufficiently rich to maintain adult interest while at the same time providing the children with learning experiences that would support all aspects of their development – oral language, early literacy, social development, and self-regulation. In other words, while parents would be exposed to the rationale for each unit as an avenue through which their children could move along the language and literacy development continuum, their children would be actively engaged in the constructive activities connected to the unit planned for their sessions. Furthermore, as parents became more aware of the significance of the features necessary for the successful development of their children, they would be better prepared to interact with their children in ways that would enhance their learning and that of their children. For example, the Creative Play Unit focused upon the parents exploring the importance of play, the relationship of play to learning in general and to literacy learning in particular, and how they could involve themselves in their children's play in supportive rather than directive ways. The children during this same period had opportunities to play alone or in groups that fostered imaginative play supported by props and literacy materials. When parents and children came together, the adults' new awareness of how children play and of how their play may be enhanced by encouraging interactions allowed the adults to offer intentional support when the need arose. In other words, the adults are much better prepared to scaffold their children's learning. It should be noted also that during adult-only sessions, adult literacy materials related to the units were woven into the curriculum so that the parents concurrently increased their own literacy abilities.

In summary, the *Learning Together* program was built upon a model of strengths. It took into consideration the social and cultural backgrounds of families and the goals of the parents. It integrated into its curriculum those elements based on evidence-based research that support positive early intervention programming. It addressed both adult and child developmental needs. It encompassed a thematic framework so that instruction would have both coherence and depth. The program offered oral language and literacy activities and procedures that parents could incorporate within the family and community to enhance and advance their own and their children's educational progress. The rationale for the program was to provide parents with the motivation and the tools to help their children; and to provide children with a learning environment that their parents could not only understand but for which they could also offer genuine support to their children's learning while concurrently advancing their own literacy abilities.

Chapter Four
Method

Pilot Study

A pilot study was conducted over a thirteen week period between January and April of 2000 (Hayden & Phillips, 2000). The aim of the pilot study was to conduct a formative evaluation of the Alberta implementation of the BSA model for family literacy programming; and to use the results from the evaluation to inform the development of a coherent, comprehensive and complete program for full implementation and intensive research and evaluation.

The report provided quantitative and qualitative findings on two family literacy program sites, one rural and one urban, and involved 17 families. Pretest and posttest data were collected on the children and their parents. Parents, program facilitators, and staff were interviewed at the beginning, the middle and end of the program. Results from the formative evaluation generally were positive. The principal findings were:

- The children's receptive vocabulary increased and they made strong gains in their knowledge of the alphabet and the conventions of print (e.g., book handling knowledge). The children's gains in their ability to construct meaning from print situations (e.g. environmental print) reflected less vigorous growth.

- The parents' ability to remember and to comprehend more accurately what they had read increased considerably, however, these improvements did not lead to an increase in reading level achievement.

- Parental views about "the what" of literacy changed from a focus on merely the learning of letters, sounds and words to one that included more strategic views of reading as the construction of meaning. Parents moved from a practice of using language primarily to regulate their children's behaviors to practices that included interactive lan-

guage use in order to address the imaginative, informational and heuristic functions of language.
- Parents perceived themselves as more confident models for the oral language and literacy development of their children.
- Parents reported the social aspects of the program to be of considerable benefit for their children and themselves.
- Staff members carried out their professional duties extremely well given the challenges faced by them as they implemented a new program.

We concluded that the *Learning Together* program adequately met two of the three program goals, namely, to boost the children's early literacy development and to assist parents in helping that development to occur. The remaining goal to increase parents' own literacy levels signaled specific advances in some aspects and not others. In conclusion, we therefore recommended that:

- In order to ensure generalizability of results, a larger sample of participants (e.g., 100 adults and 100 children) should be investigated within a *Learning Together* program in multiple urban and rural sites. A strong, robust, longitudinal study is essential in order to draw any conclusions about the program's effectiveness and generalizability.
- Instructional practices within the program need to attend more carefully to the needs and interest of boys.
- Greater attention is warranted within the curriculum and instructional practices to meaning in print development for emergent readers and writers.
- Parents need more opportunities to work on their own literacy development within the program structure.
- Those aspects of the program that appear to have worked well should be maintained.
- Staff need considerable support including more paid release time so that they may plan effectively to meet the substantial demands of program delivery.
- Every effort should be made to reach those families most in need. Working with agencies such as social services, health, and other community groups is crucial if families are to be recruited and retained in the program.

Design and Sample

The sample comprised 158 children and 156 parents on whom complete date were available at the time of the pretest. To obtain this usable sample, data were collected on 189 children and their parents in total, but 33 of the files were incomplete and not used in the following analyses. The study compared treatment groups of children and their parents to control/comparison groups of children and their parents identified by the Centre for Family Literacy.

The promotion of the *Learning Together* program, and the recruitment and retention of families for both the treatment and control groups was the sole responsibility of the Centre for Family Literacy (CFL). In consultation with the Executive Director, Maureen Sanders, the following overview lays out the process.

The recruitment of families turned out to be one of the most difficult elements of the project. This was in part due to the large time commitment required of parents for participation in the program. The registration requirements for participants were also quite narrow because of the research – children could not have previously participated in any other type of preschool program for example – and this excluded many families who responded to our recruitment efforts. Another factor was the reality that unlike other CFL programs, we could not allow for organic growth as the program became known and established, but needed to recruit quickly while the program was still relatively unknown in the communities in which it ran.

Recruitment efforts consumed large amounts of staff time in order to find families who met the criteria and who were interested in participating. A variety of promotional strategies were used, for example working through community agencies, schools, past program participants, control group participants; and using local newspapers and public service announcements on television and radio; and distributing flyers in shopping malls and at community events. Each of these strategies worked to some extent but the combination of many methods was needed to ensure a reasonable number of families for each program.

Two of the most successful approaches were (a) advertisements placed in a small community newspaper, and (b) partner agency referrals. A variety of strategies were used for recruitment through other agencies, for example:

- making contact with agency staff (via telephone, email, fax)
- attending interagency meetings

- distributing brochures, posters and information sheets to agencies over the program year.

A comparison of the actual number of contacts made as a result of promotional and recruitment efforts and the number of participants who then entered programs, shows an entry rate of approximately one participant for every five or six enquiries. During five years of programming (including programs that ran after the active research phase ended), *Learning Together* worked with well over 300 agencies and organizations for the purposes of promotion, recruitment, referrals, and support services.

Over the course of program delivery, a number of families faced significant non-literacy challenges as is usual in most literacy programs. Some of these challenges were basic needs for food, shelter, etc.; family violence; parenting issues; substance abuse; coping with a child's behavioral and developmental challenges; coming to terms with a child's special needs; family breakdown; serious health concerns; difficult pregnancies; death in the family; mental health issues; and lack of financial resources. The dropping-out that occurred in programs was usually due to one or more of these personal challenges. Coping with the non-literacy needs of participants was also a significant challenge for program staff, and they often spent time outside of their work schedule to accommodate families and to assist them in finding appropriate services.

In order to better prepare for these challenges and to ensure that families were provided with appropriate services, staff were given extra paid work hours to be able to talk individually with families and to refer them to necessary community services. As the program delivery continued, staff also received additional training in family support so that they knew how to help families in times of crisis and to ensure that families were appropriately referred.

The control group was given no treatment other than whatever families opted to do on their own prior to their children starting formal schooling. Pretests were given to all treatment children and their participating parents prior to the 13 week intervention and posttests afterwards. The same measures were used with the all control children and their participating parents at the corresponding times as the treatment groups. The same measures were used for all yearly follow-up testings for both groups.

Assessment Instruments: Children

Peabody Picture Vocabulary Test (PPVT), (3rd Ed., Forms IIIA & IIIB). The *Peabody Picture Vocabulary Test* (Dunn & Dunn, 1997) is a norm-referenced, wide-range test (2½ - 90+ years) and available in two forms IIIA and IIIB. The PPVT-III is designed to serve as an achievement test of hearing (receptive) vocabulary and as a screening test of verbal ability when English is the language of the home, the school, and the community. In the case of the former, it is in a sense an achievement test of the level of a person's vocabulary acquisition. The PPVT-III is administered individually in an untimed setting. There are a total of 204 items of increasing difficulty grouped into 17 sets of 12 items each for purposes of administration. Only the first of the six sets were given to children in this study in accord with their age, for example, Set 1, Items 1-12 are administered to three years olds. Examinees are asked to point to the picture from a set of four that best represents the meaning of the word said by the examiner. Alternate-forms reliability coefficients computed from standard scores range from .88 to .96.

Test of Early Reading Ability (TERA-2 Forms A & B), (2nd Ed.). The *Test of Early Reading Ability* (Reid, Hresko, & Hammill, 1989) is designed to measure children's ability (ages 3-9 years) to attribute meaning to printed symbols, their knowledge of the alphabet and its functions, and their understanding of the conventions of print. The *TERA* is administered individually in an untimed setting. The total number of items is 46, and these are represented as three constructs, namely, alphabet, meaning, and convention. *TERA-2* test-retest with alternate forms is reported to be .89 reliability.

Test of Early Reading Ability (TERA-3 Forms A & B), (3rd Ed.). The *Test of Early Reading Ability-3* (Reid, Hresko, & Hammill, 2001) has five purposes: (a) to identify those children who are significantly below their peers in reading development and thus may be candidates for early intervention, (b) to identify strengths and weaknesses of individual children, (c) to document children's progress as a consequence of early literacy intervention programs, (d) to serve as a measure in research studying development in young children, and (e) to accompany other assessment techniques (Examiner's Manual, p. 8).

TERA-3 is designed to measure early reading in children (ages 3-8½ years). The *TERA-3* is administered individually in an untimed setting. There are three subtests: Alphabet, Conventions, and Meaning:

Subtest I: Alphabet measures children's knowledge of the alphabet and sound-letter correspondence. It includes 29 items that measure letter-name knowledge, the ability to determine the initial and final sounds in printed words, knowledge of the number of sounds and syllables in printed words, and awareness of letters printed in different fonts.

Subtest II: Conventions measures children's familiarity with the conventions of print. It includes 21 items that measure book handling (top and bottom of a book; where to start reading), print conventions (letter orientation, case, presentation of print, text genre), and knowledge of punctuation, capitalization, and spelling.

Subtest III: Meaning measures children's ability to comprehend the meaning of printed material. It includes 30 items that measure comprehension of words, sentences, and paragraphs. Items also measure relational vocabulary, sentence construction, and paraphrasing.

The standard scores of all three subtests are combined to form the reading quotient which reflects the child's ability across a variety of reading activities and this composite score is taken to be the best indicator of overall reading ability. TERA-3 test-retest reliability with alternate forms is reported to be greater than .93 and is judged to be a valid measure of reading on the basis of correlations with other well-established tests of school achievement, confirmatory factor analysis, and item-construct validity correlations between performance on the items and total score.

Assessment Instruments: Adults

Canadian Adult Reading Assessment (CARA). The *Canadian Adult Reading Assessment* (Campbell & Brokop, 2000) is an informal reading inventory for adults. It is an individually administered placement and diagnostic instrument with two basic parts: A graded word list and graded passages including narrative and informational text. *CARA* is comprised of nine levels with readability ranging from grades 1 to 12.

Graded Word List: Performance on the graded word list is used both to identify independent reading level of isolated words and to determine the starting point for administration of the passages.

Graded Passages: Performance on the graded passages, which include informational and narrative text, coupled with a set of factual and inferential questions is used both for placement in programs and diagnosis of reading levels. In addition to oral and silent reading of the passages, adults' reading miscues, and their unaided and aided retellings provide detailed information on how they process print. Alternate-form reliability on the CARA is provided in terms of the mean absolute deviation in scores across the narrative and informational passages within each level.

The authors state that there is a high degree of alternate-form reliability and the passages are parallel in terms of difficulty (Campbell & Brokop, 2000, p. 184).

Interviews

Interviews with all treatment parents were conducted prior to and after participation in the *Learning Together* program, and for the same corresponding three-month period with all of the control parents. Yearly follow-up interviews were conducted with all families around the anniversary date of program completion.

Separate interview questionnaires were designed for each of the five data collection points in order to obtain the most pertinent information for the period of time under review. The majority of questions were open-ended thereby encouraging participants to provide greater depth to their responses. A research assistant contacted by phone or in person the adult participants in a program in order to determine a mutually convenient time and place to carry out an interview. Each interview lasted approximately one hour.

The pretest interview for the treatment parents contained 22 questions. The first six questions included the usual demographic information (age, gender, ethnicity, first language, occupational status, marital status, children's age and names, and highest level of education completed). Treatment parents were then asked six questions to describe their post-school experiences; report whether they attended any community programs; report languages spoken at home; describe their own school experiences; report the subject area(s) they felt they did not learn as well as they wished and why; and report their hobbies and interests. The remaining questions shifted to why they decided to participate in the *Learning Together* program; what they expected for their children and for themselves; what might make attendance in the program difficult; whether they had attended a similar program; what sorts of activities they do with their children; number of books at home; title of child's favorite book; how often they read to their children; the child's favorite story; how often they go to the library, go to the school to help with activities, and talk with the children's teachers; to provide an overview of the reading and writing activities for the past week; to give a sense of how they think children learn to read; and then parents were extended the opportunity to make comments or queries.

We followed the same interview schedule for the control parents as for the treatment families. The pretest interview for the control families contained 20 questions. The demographic information and the first six questions were the same, questions about the *Learning Together* program were omitted; and all other questions were the same as those asked of the treatment families.

The post-interviews for the treatment parents dealt with questions about the *Learning Together* program such as: whether they enjoyed it and why; parts enjoyed the most and why; most useful components and why; ways the programs helped their own reading and writing; what they changed about reading at home and examples; whether their children enjoyed the program and why; what they learned to help their children's reading and writing; the best part of the joint sessions; what their children can do now that they could not do before the program; whether transportation and program content had been a problem; future plans; library visits; and whether they would recommend the program to other parents.

The post-interviews for control families did not include questions about the *Learning Together* program. It included variations of the pre-test interview and included questions about what parents and their children have been doing together; things they talk about; stories they tell their children; sorts of things their child is interested in and how they encourage those interests; developmental differences noticed; and questions about their reading together.

The first, second and third follow-up annual interviews followed the same basic model as outlined for the pretest and posttest interviews for the treatment and control families. Parents were also asked where children get their books; to tell about what happens when they read together; what, how often, when, and where they read together; to tell about exciting reading and writing events in the family; sorts of things their child shows interest in; and whether they joined any community programs. The treatment parents were also asked about the influence of the *Learning Together* program on the quality of the activities they do together with their child, what they observe about their child's development, child's confidence as a reader, and questions about how we can help. Parents in the control group were asked the same questions as those in the treatment group with the exception of questions specifically dealing with the *Learning Together* program.

Observations

All program sites were visited during the joint sessions for a minimum of two hours by one of the researchers. Visits generally occurred after the mid-point of program delivery. The purpose of these visits was to determine if the rationale for the program was being actualized within the practice of the program, to determine how the content of the day's events reflected sound early intervention program practices and to observe how parents and children were interacting with one another within the prepared events.

At the beginning of each visit, the researcher (observer) had the opportunity to meet with the adult-only and early-years facilitators to talk about what was planned for the day, to obtain a lesson plan and other related materials (e.g. titles of books to be read, etc.), and to chat informally with either the children or their parents. The framework for these joint sessions usually included time for a directed activity such as a craft previously planned by the parents, time for the children to be engaged in a variety of play or "work" centres, circle time when books were read, songs sung and rhymes acted out, snack time, and private parent-child shared reading time. For example, in the creative play unit, one of the joint sessions included a directed activity where participants made a mail bag that they decorated together, wrote letters in a writing centre to a family member that they mailed in a real mail box on the way home, read several books during circle time related to mail including *Canadian Postal Workers* (Bourgeois, 1993), spent time reading together, and played in a variety of centres – blocks, puzzles, post office, etc. In short, generally the joint sessions were quite well organized while allowing for individual parent-child dyads to choose what they would do and when they would do it, with the exception of circle time when all were expected to join in together. In several joint sessions, once snack time was over and the children went to wash their hands, parents wrote what they were observing or learning about their children in their journals.

Observations of the joint sessions occurred on two levels. The first level occurred two or three times during the session at which the observer made observational sweeps of the room. That is, she wrote down what each adult and child was doing either together or alone. Once she made a notation of what an individual was doing, she turned to the next individual. These sweeps took about 10 minutes to complete. On the second level, she attended to a parent-child dyad in more detail, observing them for seven to ten minutes while writing copious notes on what was occurring and what was being said within the dyads. In order to obtain the most information possible, she had to sit near each pair while maintaining enough distance so as not to distract them. At the conclusion of each day's observation, she wrote a two to three page synopsis of her observations for later data analysis.

Chapter Five
Results and Discussion

Quantitative Analyses
Descriptive Data on Children

Table 5.1 displays the sample of children on whom complete data were available at the time they entered the study. Numbers of males and females were approximately equal within the intervention and control groups. The intervention group had about one-third more subjects than the control group. The study was conducted in five sites: three urban and two rural. One of the rural and one of the urban sites attracted very few subjects. So, although both rural and urban settings are represented, the numbers are such that rural and urban comparisons cannot be made. Also, comparisons among sites are not reported because of the very small numbers in two of them. As will be seen in subsequent analyses, there was attrition from this initial sample at the posttest and at each of the four annual follow-up data collection points.

Table 5.1
Number of Children by Site, Study Status, and Sex at Pretest

	Intervention		Control		
Site	Female	Male	Female	Male	Total
Urban 1	2	2	2	2	8
Rural 1	0	2	0	2	4
Urban 2	15	20	15	18	68
Rural 2	12	10	7	8	37
Urban 3	14	13	8	6	41
Total	43	47	32	36	158

The *Test of Early Reading Ability (TERA)* comprises three major subtests: Alphabet, Meaning, and Convention. Table 5.2 presents data on children's Alphabet scores from the pretest through the fourth follow-up. At the pretest, the control group scored slightly higher than the intervention group for both males and females. Thereafter, the control group consistently scored higher than the intervention group for the females, but only at the second follow-up for the males. At the pretest, both the males and the females averaged 45 months of age. Their pretest scores put them in the 25th to 37th percentile rank on Alphabet, meaning that 75% to 63% of children their age score higher. At the posttest, the children were four months older, and their scores put them in the same percentile ranks. At the first follow-up, children's scores placed them all at approximately the 50th percentile, and at the second follow-up between the 50th and 75th percentiles. At the third and fourth follow-ups, the children were at the

Table 5.2
TERA Alphabet Subtest Means and Standard Deviations by Study Status and Sex from Pretest to Fourth Follow-up

	Intervention		Control	
Variable	Female	Male	Female	Male
Pretest	2.7*	2.4	3.3	2.5
	(4.1)**	(3.3)	(2.9)	(4.2)
Posttest	3.8	3.6	4.2	3.2
	(4.6)	(3.6)	(4.6)	(4.4)
1st Follow-up	8.6	9.6	10.8	9.3
	(7.0)	(6.3)	(6.5)	(7.7)
2nd Follow-up	17.3	17.2	21.2	18.0
	(6.7)	(6.6)	(3.3)	(7.0)
3rd Follow-up	23.7	22.6	26.3	22.4
	(2.7)	(4.3)	(1.9)	(3.7)
4th Follow-up	27.3	24.8	28.0	24.7
	(2.4)	(2.4)	(-)***	(3.6)

*mean **SD ***only one child in this cell

25th to 75th percentile. Generally speaking, after the posttest, the group showed improvement with respect to children used as the norming sample for the test.

Figure 1 compares the distributions of the children's Alphabet scores over time and between the control and intervention groups. Note that at the pretest and posttest for both intervention and control groups the distribution is highly skewed towards the lower scores. Most of the children scored 5 or less out of a total possible score of 29, meaning that most children had difficulty differentiating the letters of the alphabet from numbers or designs and naming the letters of the alphabet. At the first and second follow-ups, there is a fairly even distribution of scores from the lowest to the mid-20s. At the third follow-up, the distribution is skewed in the opposite direction, with hardly any child scoring below 15, meaning that many of the children were able to isolate beginning, middle, and ending sounds; to discern the number of sounds and syllables in a word; and to recognize some words by sight.

Table 5.3 presents data on children's Convention scores from the pretest to the fourth follow-up. As with Alphabet scores, the control group scored higher than the intervention group at the pretest both for males and females. At the posttest and fourth follow-up, the intervention group scored higher than the control group. For the first through third follow-up, the control group tended to score higher. At the pretest, the percentile ranking of the group is the same as for Alphabet, 25th to 37th. At the posttest and first follow-up, the percentile ranking on the Convention subtest is from the 37th to 50th. For the first follow-up, the ranking was from the 25th to the 75th percentiles, and for the third follow-up from the 25th to 63rd percentiles. As with Alphabet, the children's Convention scores were generally higher compared to the norming sample for tests taken after the pretest.

Figure 2 displays the distributions of children's Convention scores. At the pretest and third follow-up, we see skewing similar to that found with the Alphabet scores, and at the first and second follow-ups, the scores are fairly evenly distributed across the entire range as also was the case for the Alphabet scores. At the posttest, although the scores are mostly confined to the lower half of the scale, there is not the pronounced skewing that was found in the case of the Alphabet scores. This result means that there were fewer children who knew none or hardly any text conventions than who knew none or hardly any letters.

Table 5.4 provides data on Meaning from the pretest to fourth follow-up. As with the other two subtests, the control group for both males and females scored higher than the intervention group at the pretest. For sub-

54 Family Literacy Matters

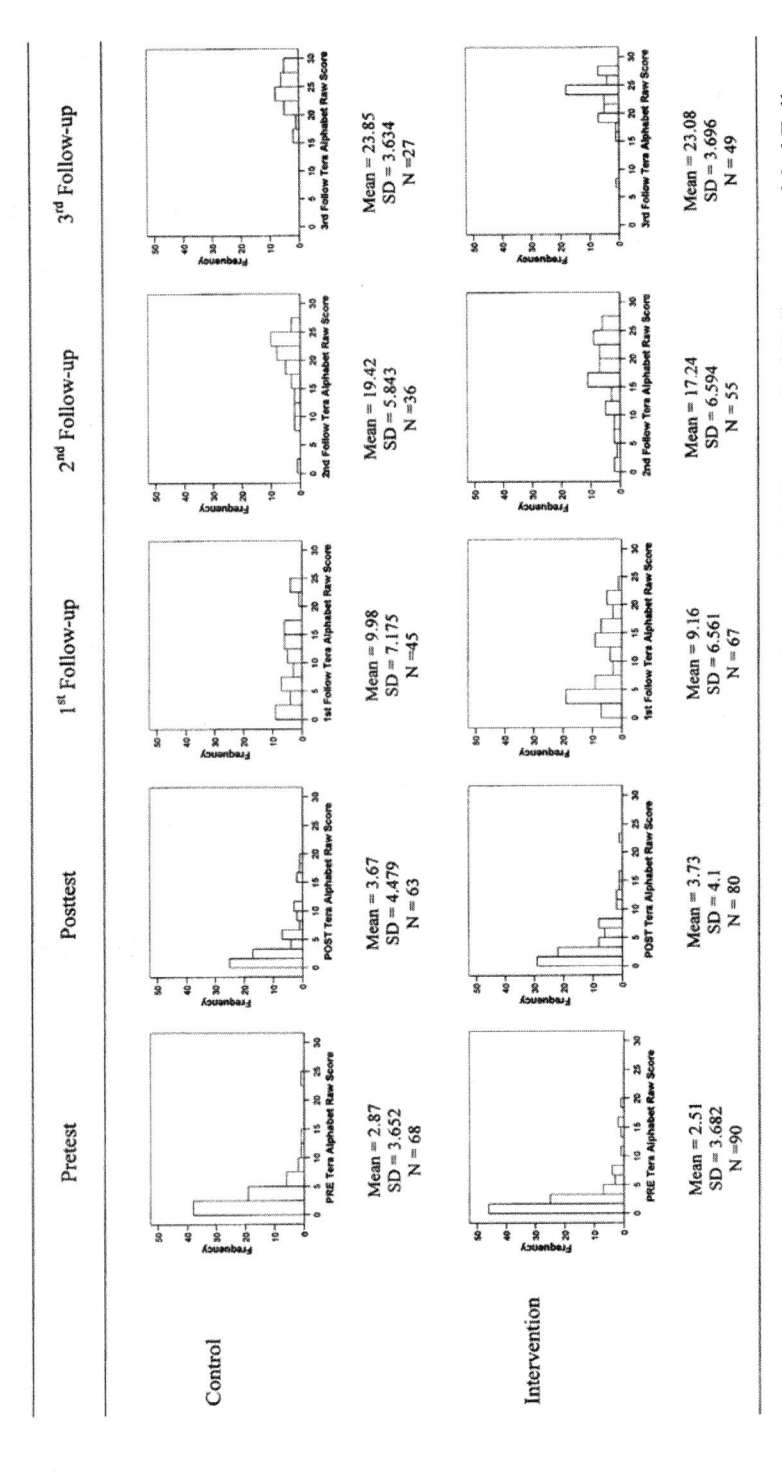

Figure 1. Histograms for the TERA Alphabet Subtest Raw Scores at Pretest, Posttest, 1st Follow-up, 2nd Follow-up, and 3rd Follow-up

Table 5.3
TERA Convention Subtest Means and Standard Deviations by Study Status and Sex from Pretest to Fourth Follow-up

	Intervention		Control	
Variable	Female	Male	Female	Male
Pretest	1.4*	1.2	2.1	1.6
	(2.0)**	(1.8)	(1.9)	(2.1)
Posttest	4.0	3.3	3.5	3.0
	(2.8)	(2.5)	(2.9)	(2.5)
1st Follow-up	6.8	6.0	7.5	6.8
	(3.9)	(3.7)	(4.3)	(4.3)
2nd Follow-up	11.1	10.7	14.1	10.7
	(4.0)	(4.8)	(3.1)	(4.9)
3rd Follow-up	15.4	14.9	17.0	15.3
	(3.5)	(3.4)	(1.9)	(2.8)
4th Follow-up	18.5	18.2	18.0	17.8
	(2.4)	(1.8)	(-)***	(3.1)

*Mean   **SD   ***only one child in this cell

sequent testings, the females in the control group scored higher than those in the intervention group, while the males in the control group scored either lower or the same as the males in the intervention group. The percentile ranking at the pretest was the same as for the other two subtests, 25th to 37th. At subsequent testings, the percentile ranks were generally higher, except at the posttest: posttest, 16th to 25th; first follow-up, 50th to 63rd; second follow-up, 37th to 50th; third follow-up, 16th to 63rd; and fourth follow-up, 25th to 63rd.

The distribution of Meaning scores displayed in Figure 3 shows, at least up to and including the second follow-up, a greater tendency compared to the Alphabet and Convention subtests for scores to coalesce around a mean, which a relatively higher number of students attained, and to drop off in frequency on either side of that mean. The exception lies in the third follow-up, where scores distribute relatively evenly across the upper two-thirds or so of the scale.

56 Family Literacy Matters

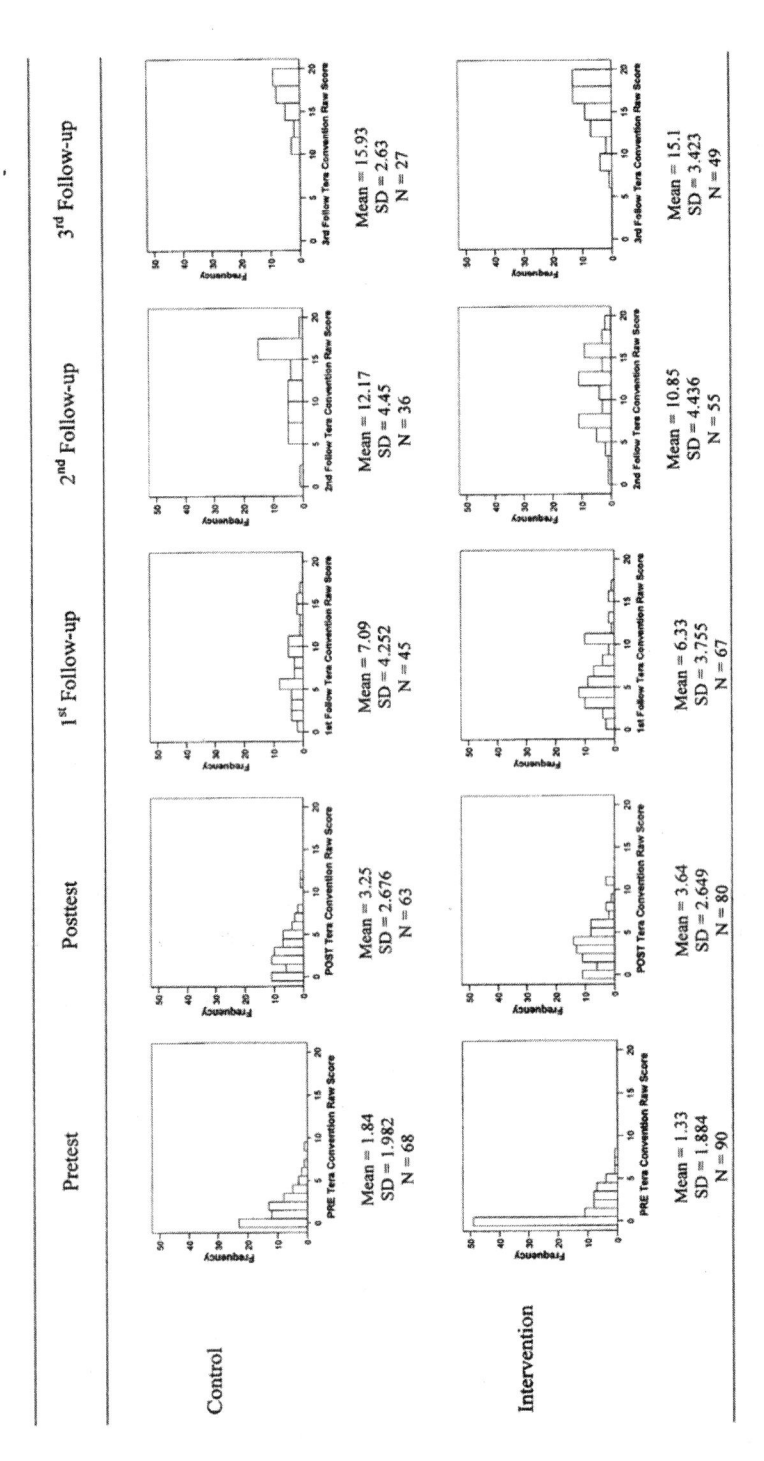

Figure 2. Histograms for the TERA Convention Subtest Raw Scores at Prettest, Posttest, 1st Follow-up, 2nd Follow-up, and 3rd Follow-up

Table 5.4
TERA Meaning Subtest Means and Standard Deviations by Study Status and Sex from Pretest to Fourth Follow-up

	Intervention		Control	
Variable	Female	Male	Female	Male
Pretest	4.4*	4.1	5.4	4.9
	(2.5)**	(2.3)	(2.0)	(2.5)
Posttest	5.5	4.6	5.8	4.6
	(3.1)	(2.8)	(3.4)	(3.0)
1st Follow-up	8.9	9.4	9.7	9.0
	(3.4)	(2.7)	(2.1)	(2.9)
2nd Follow-up	11.3	12.6	13.0	12.6
	(3.5)	(5.0)	(5.8)	(5.7)
3rd Follow-up	17.6	16.5	23.1	15.4
	(6.3)	(6.1)	(4.9)	(7.3)
4th Follow-up	21.5	21.9	27.0	21.7
	(6.5)	(7.6)	(-)***	(7.3)

*Mean   **SD   ***only one child in this cell

Table 5.5 shows *TERA* total scores, which are simply the sum of the three subtest scores, as the children grew from an average age of 3 years 9 months to 8 years 1 month. At the 8 years 1 month point, their scores put them at approximately the 45th percentile, which places the group of children as a whole at about the average for the comparison group. Figure 4 shows the distribution of TERA total scores. As expected, because these graphs combine the results of the three subtests, there is a reduction in the radical skewing seen with some of the subtest scores and a greater tendency for there to be even distributions around a central mean.

Table 5.6 provides PPVT scores from the pretest to the fourth follow-up for males and females and intervention and control groups. The control group scored higher than the intervention group at the pretest and at most subsequent testings. At the pretest and posttest stages, the percentile rankings of the children's scores ranged from 39th to 50th. Thereafter, their scores increased into the 58th to 75th percentile rankings. Figure 5 shows

58 Family Literacy Matters

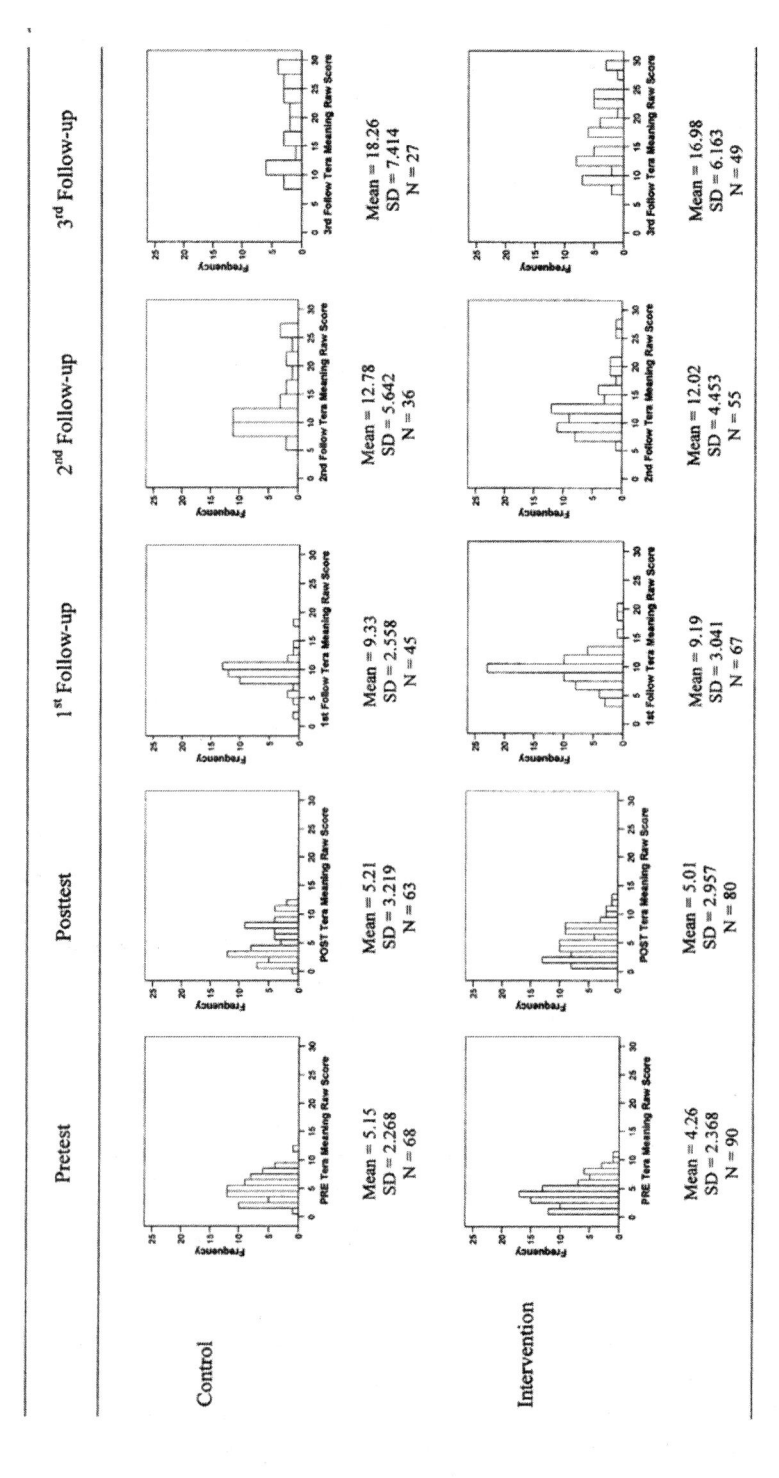

Figure 3. Histograms for the TERA Meaning Subtest Raw Scores at Pretest, Posttest, 1st Follow-up, 2nd Follow-up, and 3rd Follow-up

the distribution of the scores at each point in time. Unlike with some of the TERA subtests, there was little skewing of the distributions evident.

Table 5.5
TERA Total Score Means and Standard Deviations by Study Status and Sex from Pretest to Fourth Follow-up

	Intervention		Control	
Variable	Female	Male	Female	Male
Pretest	8.5*	7.9	10.8	9.0
	(7.2)**	(6.5)	(5.5)	(7.6)
Posttest	13.3	11.5	13.6	10.8
	(9.2)	(7.5)	(8.9)	(8.5)
1st Follow-up	24.2	25.1	28.1	25.1
	(12.8)	(10.7)	(11.4)	(13.2)
2nd Follow-up	39.7	40.4	48.3	41.3
	(12.2)	(14.9)	(10.6)	(16.2)
3rd Follow-up	56.7	54.0	66.4	53.1
	(11.7)	(12.1)	(6.7)	(12.4)
4th Follow-up	67.3	64.9	73.0	64.1
	(10.7)	(10.2)	(-)***	(11.8)

*Mean   **SD   ***only one child in this cell

60 Family Literacy Matters

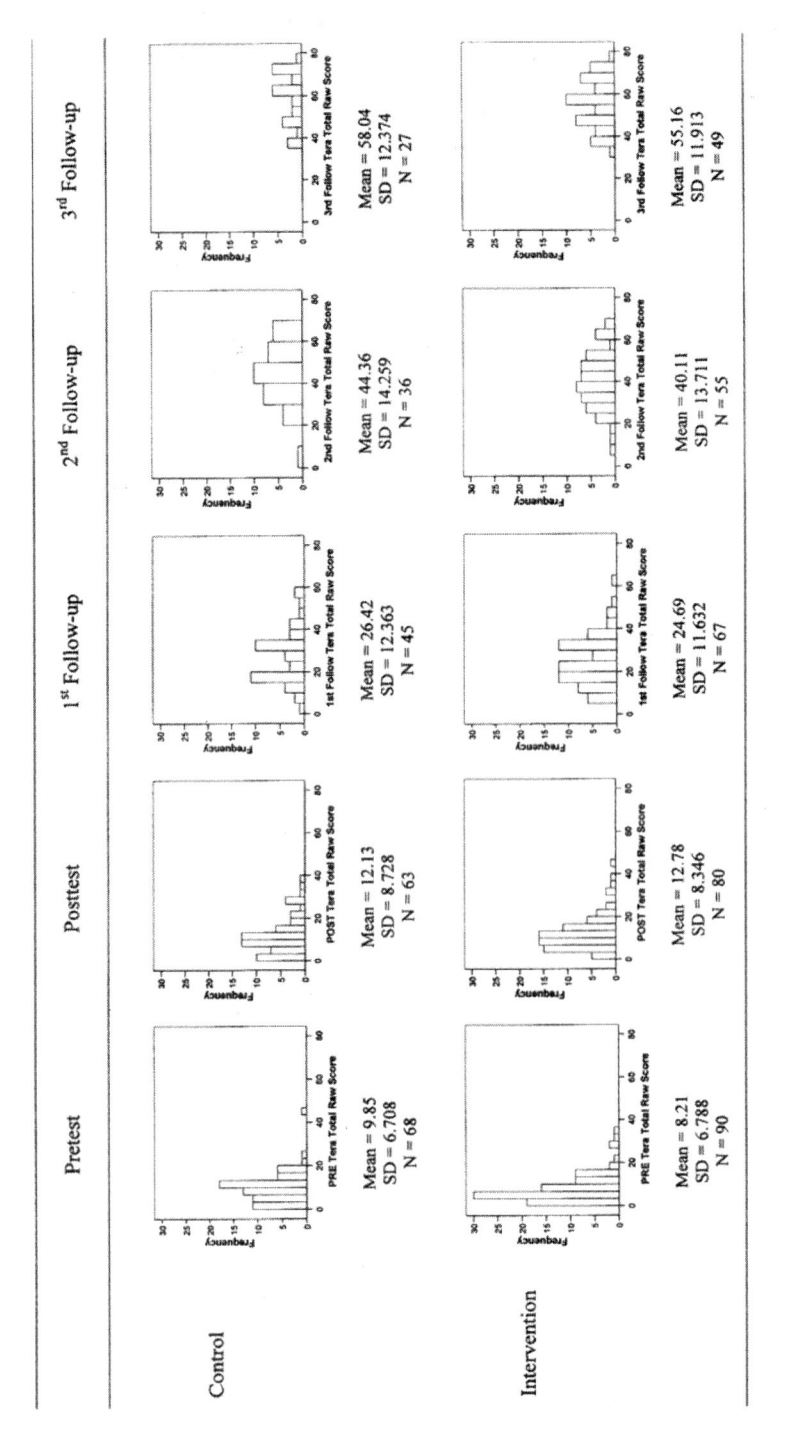

Figure 4. Histograms for the TERA Total Raw Scores at Pretest, Posttest, 1st Follow-up, 2nd Follow-up, and 3rd Follow-up

Table 5.6
Peabody Total Score Means and Standard Deviations by Study Status and Sex from Pretest to Fourth Follow-up

	Intervention		Control	
Variable	Female	Male	Female	Male
Pretest	42.7*	40.5	48.2	42.9
	(21.0)**	(22.5)	(20.4)	(18.1)
Posttest	50.1	47.5	54.3	48.8
	(19.9)	(21.3)	(16.1)	(16.5)
1st Follow-up	69.5	70.9	76.5	68.6
	(29.8)	(24.7)	(21.9)	(20.8)
2nd Follow-up	86.1	87.8	97.1	90.8
	(18.7)	(22.6)	(18.0)	(15.0)
3rd Follow-up	100.4	99.9	105.3	107.4
	(20.9)	(22.4)	(17.7)	(13.5)
4th Follow-up	108.3	119.5	114.0	120.9
	(20.9)	(19.9)	(-)***	(14.2)

*Mean   **SD   ***only one child in this cell

62 *Family Literacy Matters*

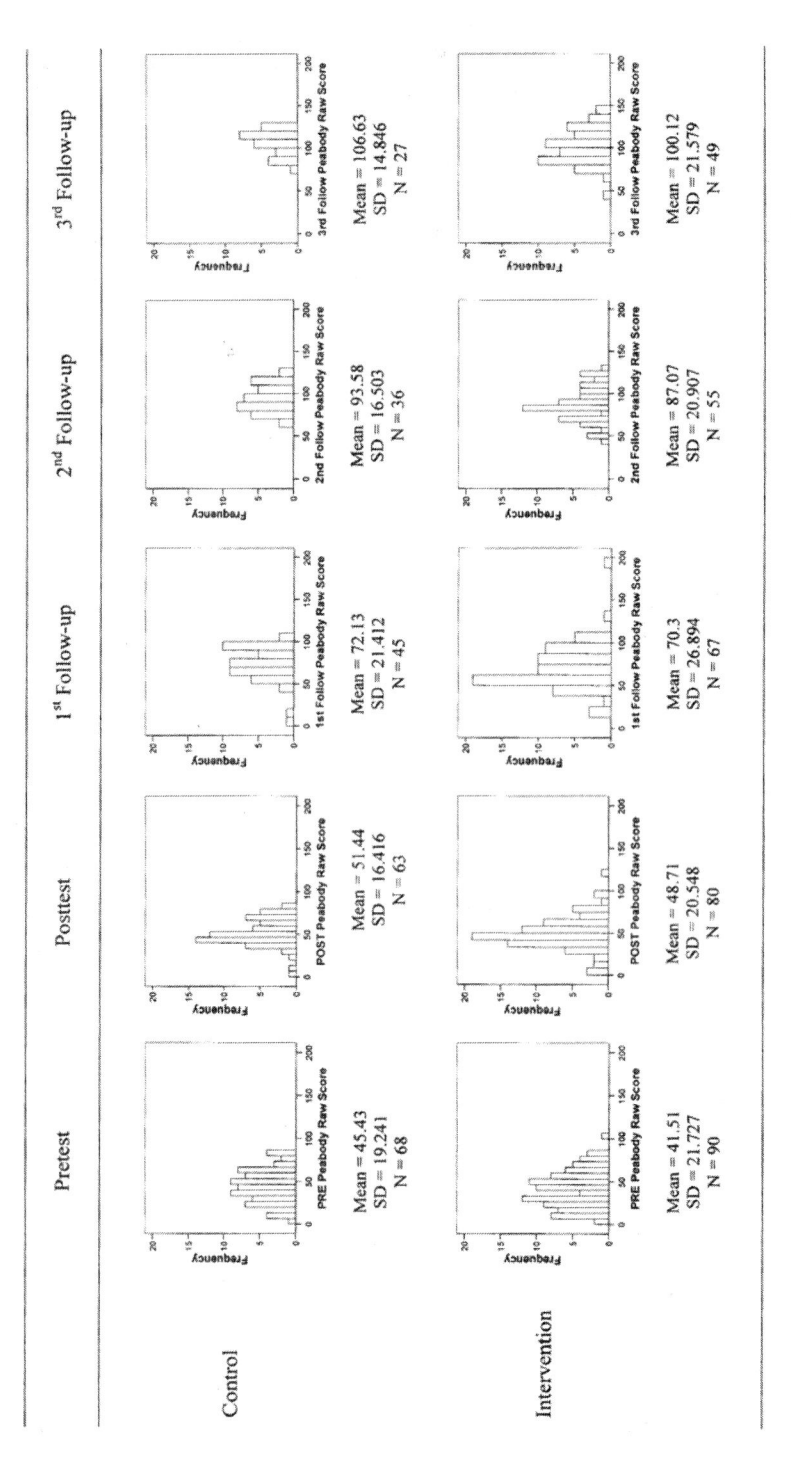

Figure 5. Histograms for the Peabody Raw Scores at Pretest, Posttest, 1st Follow-up, 2nd Follow-up, and 3rd Follow-up

Descriptive Data on Parents

Figures 6 to 13 display demographic data on the children's parents or primary caregivers at the time that they entered the study. Their ages ranged from 20 to 64 years with an average of approximately 31 years. In response to an open-ended request for ethnicity, 20 groups were named, with approximately 65% being Caucasian, approximately 16% being Aboriginal, 4% being Chinese, and the remainder representing 2% or fewer of the sample. The number of children ranged from 1 to 8, with a mean of 2.5. The five categories of marital status included 61% married, 18% single, 14% common law, 5% separated, and 3% divorced. Employment status showed 32% employed full- or part-time, and 68% unemployed. Educational levels ranged from third grade to at least some university. Approximately 15% had no high school education, another 28% had some high school education, 55% had graduated from high school, and about 1% had some university education. There were 20 first languages spoken in the group with English being the most common at about 76% and all other languages at less than 3% of the sample.

The CARA Graded Passage scale includes nine levels covering first to twelfth grade. As shown in Figure 13, approximately 22% obtained level 9, which represents high school advanced level performance. Another 22% performed at an upper fundamental or a junior high school level. Approximately 23% performed at a beginner fundamental level or a level less than that expected of those with an elementary school education. Another approximately 33% performed at an intermediate or upper elementary school level. Table 5.7 displays descriptive statistics on the CARA Graded Passage scores. At each point in the study, some parents scored the minimum and some the maximum, and the mean score varied little from one testing to the other. A mean score of 7 is at the upper fundamental level.

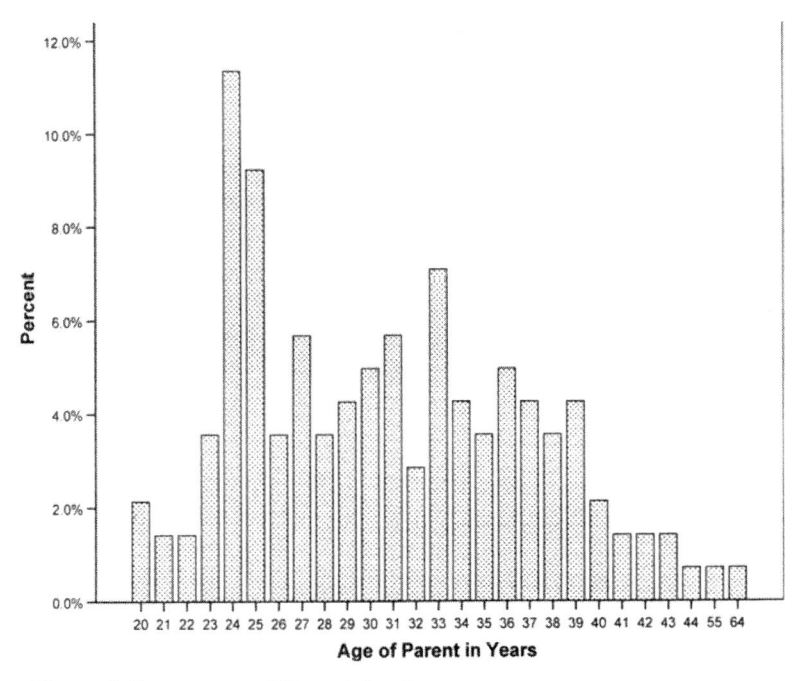

Figure 6. Percentage of Parents by Age

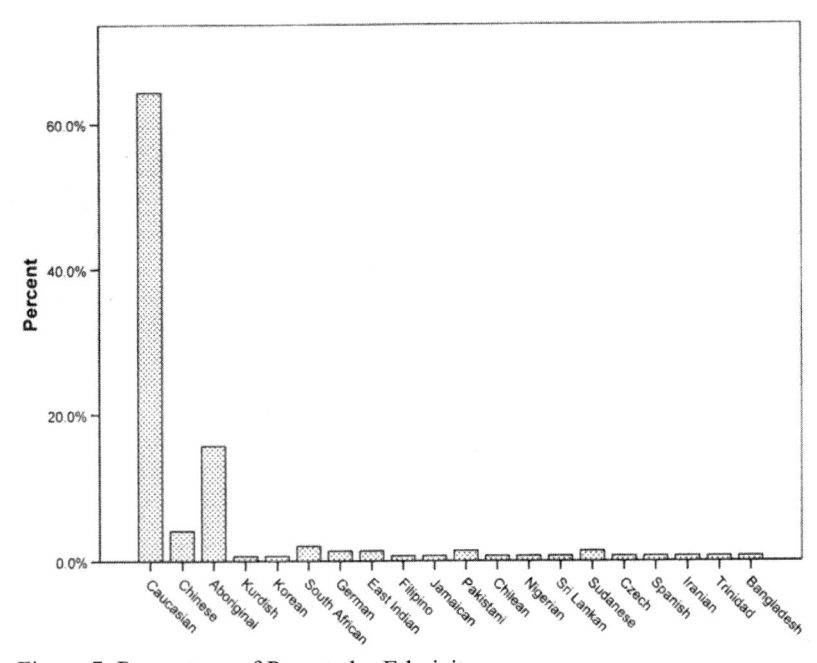

Figure 7. Percentage of Parents by Ethnicity

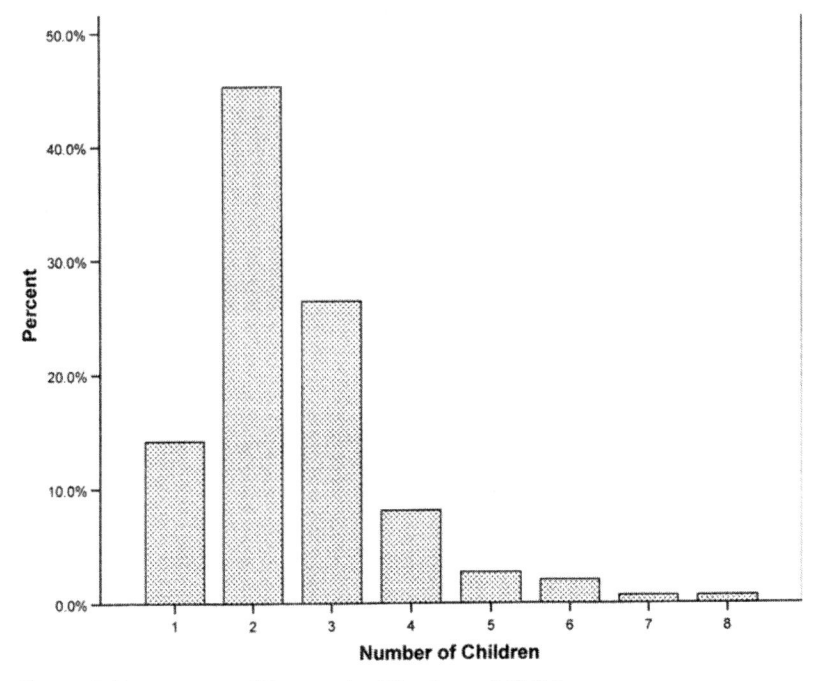

Figure 8. Percentage of Parents by Number of Children

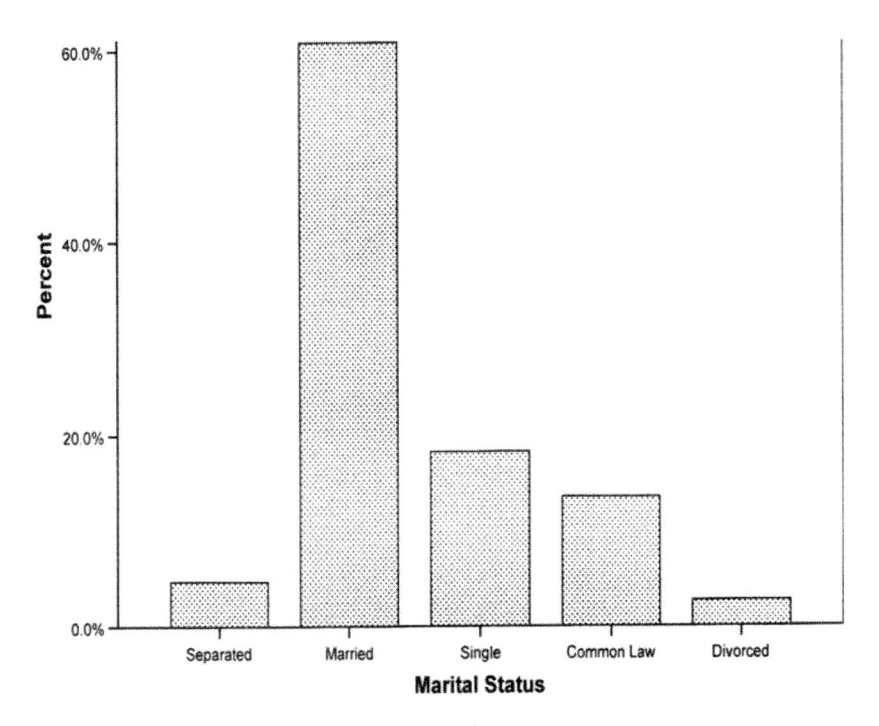

Figure 9. Percentage of Parents by Marital Status

66 *Family Literacy Matters*

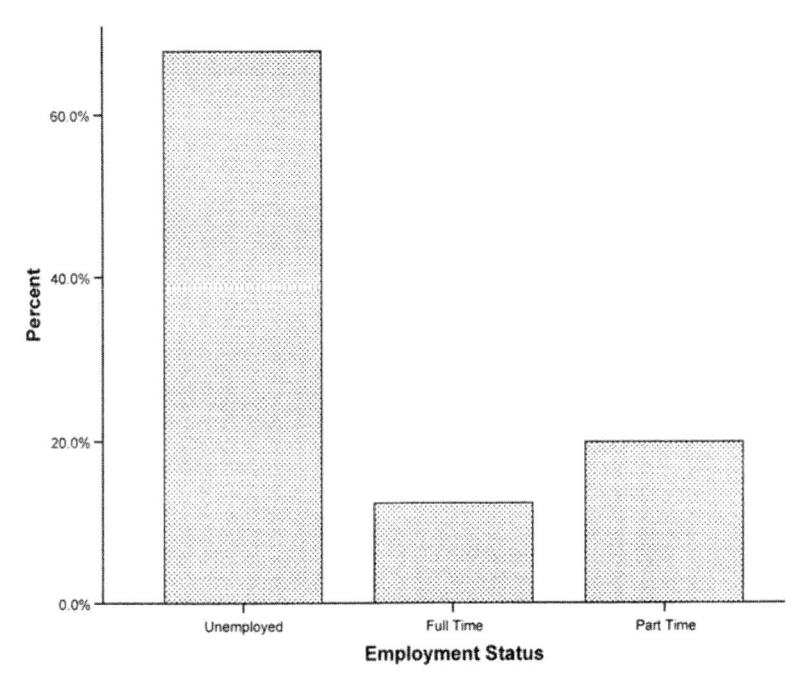

Figure 10. Percentage of Parents by Employment Status

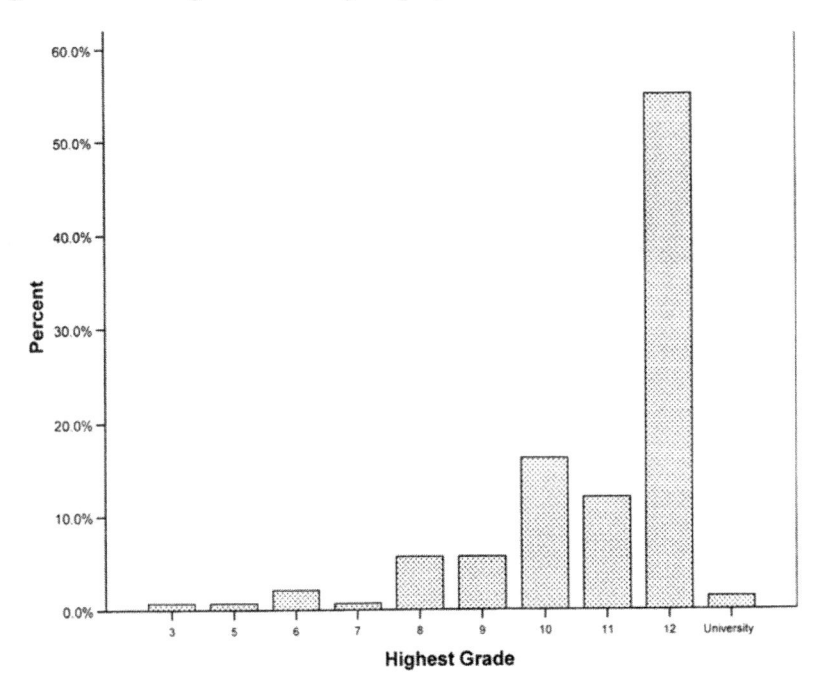

Figure 11. Percentage of Parents by Highest Grade Completed

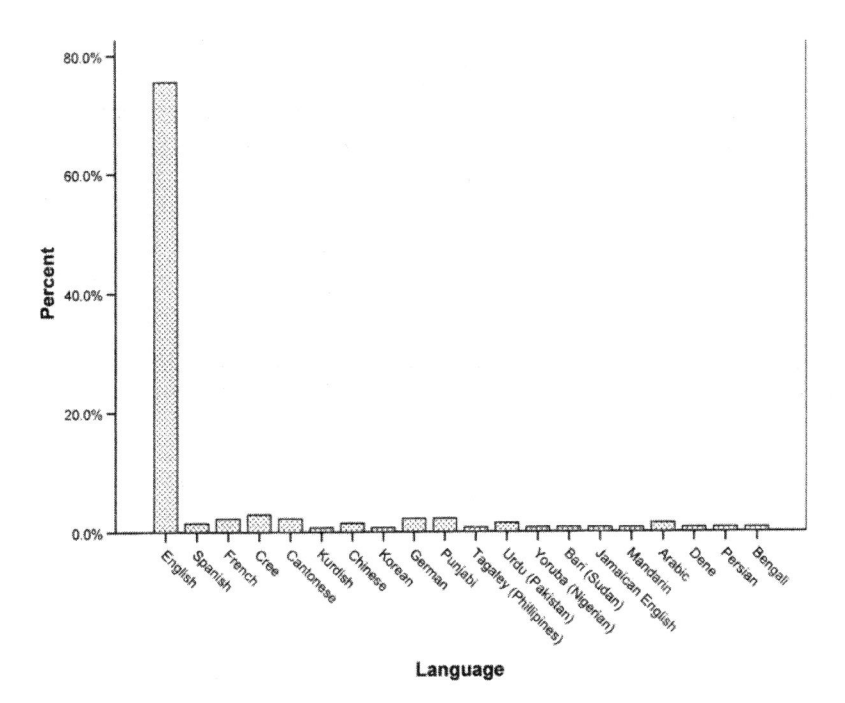

Figure 12. Percentage of Parents by First Language

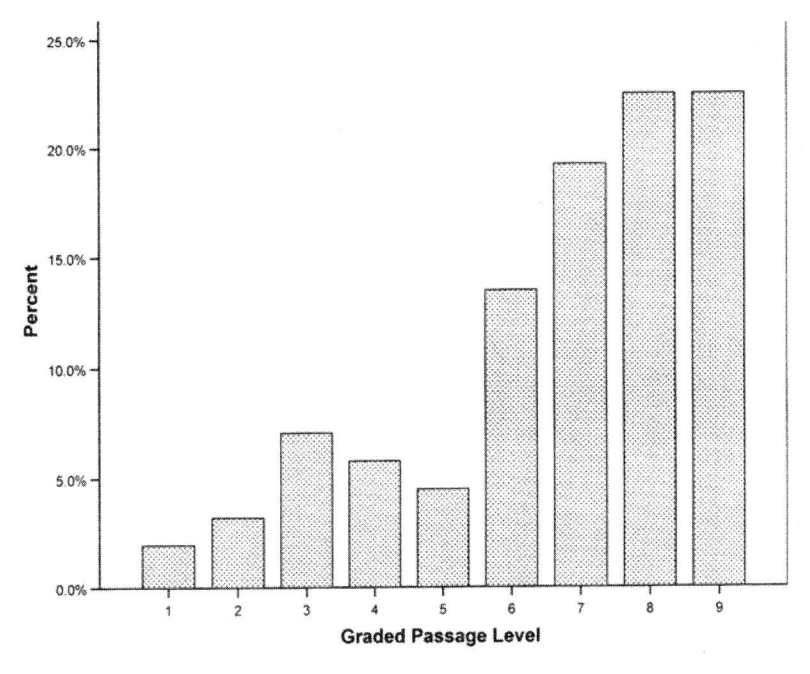

Figure 13. Percentage of Parents at Each Graded Passage Level

Table 5.7
Number of Parents, Minimum and Maximum Scores, Means and Standard Deviations for CARA Graded Passage at Each Point in the Study

Variable	N	Minimum	Maximum	Mean	SD
Pretest	156	1	9	6.72	2.13
Posttest	141	1	9	6.84	2.08
1st Follow-up	108	1	9	7.08	1.94
2nd Follow-up	81	1	9	7.01	2.06
3rd Follow-up	72	1	9	7.33	2.14
4th Follow-up	22	1	9	6.82	2.59

Effects of Parents' Characteristics on Children's Initial Literacy Achievement

We modeled mathematically with regression equations children's pretest TERA and PPVT scores, as dependent variables, using their parents' characteristics as independent variables. In the case of TERA, the parent variables that correlated significantly with the pretest were educational level, first language, and their CARA Graded Passage level at the pretest. For the PPVT, the correlated variables also included ethnicity and number of children. Initial regression models were tested using all of the variables that were significantly correlated with the dependent variables.

With TERA, first language was found to be an insignificant and the least powerful of the three predictors and was removed from the model. Model I was statistically significant (p < .001) and accounted for 13% of the variance in children's TERA pretest score:

MODEL I:

TERA Pretest = 6.21 + 2.00 (SOME HIGH SCHOOL)
              + 3.94 (HIGH SCHOOL OR GREATER)
              + 0.77 (CARA GRADED PASSAGE Pretest)

In Model I, either having some high school education or having a high school education or greater are both compared to having no high school education at all. Also, the CARA Graded Passage Pretest scores have been centred around the mean of 6.72 by subtracting the 6.72 from each parent's score. The model should be interpreted as follows:

6.21 = TERA Pretest score for children whose parents have no high school education, and have an average (i.e., 6.72) CARA Graded Passage Pretest score

2.00 = increase in TERA Pretest scores for children when their parents have *some high school education* and an average CARA Graded Passage Pretest score

3.94 = increase in TERA Pretest scores for children when their parents have a *high school education or greater* and an average CARA Graded Passage Pretest score

0.77 = increase in TERA Pretest scores for children when their parents have no high school education and their *CARA Graded Passage Pretest score increases by 1 score level.*

According to Model I, a child whose parents have high school or greater education and whose score is the maximum (i.e., 9) on the CARA Graded Passage Pretest should expect a TERA Pretest score of 11.91, compared to a child whose parents have no high school education and score the minimum on the CARA Graded Passage who should expect a score of 1.81. To put this increase of 10.1 points in perspective, a child of average age in this sample (3 years and 9 months) who scored 11.91 on the test would be in the 92nd percentile, while an average aged child with a score of 1.8 would be at about the 20th percentile. These results show the incredibly powerful combined effect of parents' education and parents' reading ability on their children's reading ability before entering school.

Effects of Parents' Characteristics on Their Own CARA Graded Passage Score

Having seen in Model I the powerful effect of parents' reading ability on their children's preschool reading ability, we explored models to explain parents' reading ability. The model we report here used parents' age, their ethnicity, their educational level, and their first language to predict their CARA Graded Passage Pretest score. The model accounted for 35% of the variance in the Graded Passage score ($p < .001$).

MODEL II:

CARA GRADED PASSAGE Pretest
  = 5.29 − 0.03 (PARENTS' AGE)
    − 0.85 (ABORIGINAL ETHNICITY)
    − 1.54 (OTHER ETHNICITY)
    + 0.89 (SOME HIGH SCHOOL)
    + 1.60 (HIGH SCHOOL OR GREATER)
    + 0.87 (ENGLISH FIRST LANGUAGE)

In Model II, parents' age is centred around the mean of 31 years (by subtracting 31 from all ages); aboriginal and other ethnicity are compared to Caucasian; some high school education and high school education or greater are compared to no high school education at all; and English as a first language is compared to all 19 other languages. The model should be interpreted as follows:

5.29 = CARA Graded Passage Pretest score for parents of average age
  (i.e., 31 years), Caucasian, with no high school education, and who
  do not have English as their first language

-0.03 = decrease in CARA Graded Passage Pretest score for *every year older* for parents who are Caucasian, have no high school education, and who do not have English as their first language

-0.85 = decrease in CARA Graded Passage Pretest score for parents of average age, who are *Aboriginal*, have no high school education, and who do not have English as their first language

-1.54 = decrease in CARA Graded Passage Pretest score for parents of average age, whose *ethnicity is other than Aboriginal,* have no high school education, and who do not have English as their first language

0.89 = increase in CARA Graded Passage Pretest score for parents of average age, who are Caucasian, have *some high school education*, and who do not have English as their first language

1.60 = increase in CARA Graded Passage Pretest score for parents of average age, who are Caucasian, have *high school education or greater,* and who do not have English as their first language

0.87 = increase in CARA Graded Passage Pretest score for parents of average age, who are Caucasian, have no high school education, and who have English as their first language

According to Model II, a parent of average age who is Caucasian, has a high school education or greater, and has English as a first language can expect a CARA Graded Passage Pretest score of 7.76. By comparison, a parent of average age, who is not Caucasian and whose ethnicity is other than Aboriginal, and who has no high school education and a first language other than English, can expect a CARA Graded Passage Pretest score of 3.75. These differences are qualitatively significant, marking a difference between a person reading at the junior high school level compared to one reading at the early elementary school level.

The only factor in Model II contributing to parents' reading level over which parents have any control is their education. The education factor can cancel out the negative effects of ethnicity, bringing parents' reading levels to the upper elementary school level. Such a change in parents' reading level could, according to Model I, increase their children's reading scores by more than 1 point on the TERA scale, which would mean as much as 10 to 15 points on the percentile scale and constitute a very significant increase.

Effects of Intervention on Children's Literacy Achievement

We explored a variety of models using the TERA and PPVT Pretest scores, the children's age, their sex, and whether they were in the intervention or control group to predict their TERA and PPVT scores at various points in the study. We found that the children's sex was not a significant factor influencing their reading scores for either the TERA or the PPVT, so we eliminated it from our final models. We also tested a variety of additive and interactive models. We report the interactive models when they accounted for a significantly greater proportion of the variance in the dependent variables. In an interactive model, the effect of an independent variable on a dependent variable differs depending upon the value of a third variable. For example, we tested whether the effect of the intervention on posttest scores differed depending upon the ages of the children. In an additive model, the effects of each independent variable can be considered separately and not to depend upon the values of the other variables. We first report the models for TERA, and thereafter those for PPVT.

MODEL III:

TERA Posttest = 10.81 + 0.96 (TERA Pretest)
  + 0.23 (AGE)
  + 2.03 (INTERVENTION)

In Model III, TERA Pretest is used as a covariate to take into account any differences between the reading levels of children in the control and intervention groups at the pretest stage. The TERA Pretest scores are centred around the mean for the group of 8.92. Age also is centred around the mean, which was 44.66 months. The model compares the intervention group to the control and accounts for 74% ($p < .001$) of the variance in the TERA Posttest score. The model should be interpreted as follows:

10.81 = TERA Posttest score for children with an average TERA Pretest score (i.e., 8.92), average age at the beginning of the study (i.e., 44.66 months), and in the control group

0.96 = increase in TERA Posttest score for *every increase of 1.0 in TERA Pretest score* for children of average age and in the control group

0.23 = increase in TERA Posttest score for *every increase of 1 month in age* for children with average TERA Pretest scores and in the control group

2.03 = increase in TERA Posttest scores for children with an average
TERA Pretest score, average age, and *in the intervention group*

Thus, comparing children of average age and average TERA Pretest scores, those in the control could expect a score of 10.81 and those in the intervention group a score of 12.84. This increase is equivalent to moving from about the 65th percentile to about the 72nd percentile.

The subsequent models from the 1st to 3rd follow-up TERA scores are all interactive, because they accounted for more variance than the additive models. The centering of variables as described for Model III continues.

MODEL IV:

TERA 1st FOLLOW-UP
= 24.14 + 1.29 (TERA Pretest)
+ 0.55 (AGE)
+ 1.60 (INTERVENTION)
− 0.50 (TERA Pretest) (INTERVENTION)

Model IV accounts for 53% ($p < .001$) of the variance in TERA 1st Follow-up. Rather than interpret all of the coefficients as we have done for previous models, we compare how the model works for the children in the control and intervention groups. For the intervention group, the model stands as above. For the control group, the model reduces as follows:

MODEL IV (Control Group only):

TERA 1st FOLLOW-UP = 24.14 + 1.29 (TERA Pretest)
+ 0.55 (AGE)

Comparing both models, it can be seen that the intervention group outperformed the control group if and only if [1.60(INTERVENTION) − 0.50 (TERA Pretest) (Intervention)] > 0, which is true, if and only if TERA Pretest < 3.20. Recall that centred scores are being used, so this result means that the intervention was beneficial for children whose TERA Pretest scores were less than 3.2 points above the mean or less than 12.91. Close to 79% of the children scored less than this value. To help put this finding in perspective, for the children of average age with the lowest TERA Pretest score of 1.0 who were in the intervention group, their TERA Posttest scores were boosted by an amount equivalent to 1.60

− (0.50)(−7.92) = 5.56. This boost changed their TERA 1st Follow-up score from 13.92 to 19.48, or from the 16th to the 35th percentile. For the children whose TERA Pretest scores were average, their boost was 1.60, or from 24.14 to 25.74, which is about a 11 percentile point change from the 50th to 61st percentile. The boost was greatest for those starting at the lowest reading levels and diminished as TERA Pretest scores increased, up to a score of 12.91, after which the children in the intervention group did not benefit.

The interactive models for the 2nd and 3rd follow-ups accounted for significantly more variance than the additive models, so the interactive models are reported here.

> MODEL V (accounting for 50% of the variance in TERA, $p < .001$):
> TERA 2nd FOLLOW-UP
> = 39.05 + 1.34 (TERA Pretest)
> + 0.85 (AGE)
> + 2.27 (INTERVENTION)
> − 0.75 (TERA Pretest) (INTERVENTION)

Model V means the children in the intervention group outperformed those in the control group if and only if their TERA Pretest scores were less than 11.95. About 78% of children scored lower than this value. The boost from the intervention for the lowest performing children of average age on TERA Pretest was 8.21, or from a score of 28.44 to 36.65, that is, from the 10th to the 39th percentile. For the children of average age and average TERA Pretest scores, their boost from the intervention was from 39.05 to 41.32, or from the 39th to the 45th percentiles.

Model VI means the children in the intervention group outperformed those in the control group if and only if their TERA Pretest scores were less than 10.36, or about 70% of the children. The boost for children of average age and with the lowest performance on the TERA Pretest was 8.14, from a score of 45.63 to 53.77, from the 8th to the 23rd percentile.

> MODEL VI (accounting for 38% of the variance in TERA, $p < .001$):
> TERA 3rd FOLLOW-UP
> = 55.13 + 1.20 (TERA Pretest)
> + 0.69 (AGE)
> + 1.25 (INTERVENTION)
> − 0.87 (TERA Pretest) (INTERVENTION)

We thus conclude that the effects of the intervention up to and including the 3rd follow-up depend upon the beginning reading levels of the children. The intervention benefited those children in the bottom 70% to 80% of the sample on the TERA Pretest. Those in the top 20% to 30% did not benefit from the intervention and likely would have profited from a more advanced program.

For the fourth follow-up, we return to an additive model to account for the TERA 4th Follow-up scores.

MODEL VII (accounting for 36% of the variance in TERA, $p < .03$):

TERA 4th FOLLOW-UP = 65.96 + 0.88 (TERA Pretest)
  + 0.74 (AGE)
  + 3.88 (INTERVENTION)

Although the overall model is significant, the effect of the intervention is not, even though its coefficient seems large when compared to the previous models. The significant factors predicting TERA 4th follow-up are age and the TERA Pretest. At this point in the study, the number of children remaining was small (23) and statistically significant results thus more difficult to obtain.

The best models for predicting the PPVT posttest and follow-up scores differed from those for TERA. First, although in the case of TERA, interactive models tended to predict better than additive models, for the PPVT additive models worked better overall. Second, whereas in the TERA models, children's age was always a significant predictor of the TERA posttest and follow-up scores, in the PPVT models age was a significant predictor only up until the first follow-up. Third, whereas in the TERA models the intervention had either an overall significant effect on TERA posttest scores, or an interactive effect conditioned on TERA pretest scores, in the case of PPVT no effects of the intervention were found.

MODEL VIII (accounting for 64% of the variance in Peabody, $p < .001$):

Peabody Posttest = 49.64 + 0.60 (Peabody Pretest)
  + 0.53 (AGE)
  + 0.74 (INTERVENTION)

The expected score of 49.64 for a student with an average PPVT Pretest score, average age, and in the control group would place that student at the 21st percentile. The strongest predictor for the posttest score was the pretest. For every 1.00 increase in the PPVT Pretest, we would expect a student of average age to experience a 0.60 increase in the PPVT posttest. Thus, the spread of 102 points from the lowest to the highest PPVT pretest score accounts for about 60 points, or nearly one-half of the total spread in PPVT posttest scores, which was 124 points. Age, which is a significant predictor in Model VIII, accounts for another 15 points of the spread in points on the PPVT posttest scores at 0.53 of a point for every increase in age of 1.0 months.

MODEL IX (accounting for 55% of the variance in Peabody, p < .001):

Peabody 1st Follow-up = 67.47 + 0.68 (Peabody Pretest)
              + 0.83 (AGE)
              + 5.56 (INTERVENTION)

In Model IX, the strengths of both the PPVT Pretest and Age increase as predictors of the PPVT 1st follow-up, with age yielding over 0.80 points increase on the 1st follow-up score for each increase of 1.0 month in age at the beginning of the study. In the subsequent three models, X to XII, only the PPVT Pretest score is a significant predictor of the follow-up scores. Even so, the pretest score in each case accounts for a considerable proportion of the variance in the follow-up scores.

MODEL X (accounting for 74% of the variance in Peabody, p < .001):

Peabody 2nd Follow-up = 87.11 + 0.78 (Peabody Pretest)
              + 0.02 (AGE)
              + 2.48 (INTERVENTION)

MODEL XI (accounting for 54% of the variance in Peabody, p < .001):

Peabody 3rd Follow-up = 101.94 + 0.73 (Peabody Pretest)
              − 0.39 (AGE)
              + 0.38 (INTERVENTION)

> MODEL XII (accounting for 53% of the variance in Peabody, $p < .002$):
>
> Peabody 4th Follow-up = 119.49 + 0.56 (Peabody Pretest)
> + 0.33 (AGE)
> − 1.32 (INTERVENTION)

At each of the follow-up points, the percentile ranks for a student with an average PPVT Pretest score, average age, and in the control group would be: 2nd follow-up, 61st percentile; 3rd follow-up, 61st percentile; and 4th follow-up, 68th percentile. For the average student in the sample, these scores are very respectable, placing the student well above half of those in the comparison group used to construct the PPVT norms.

Effects of Intervention on Parents' Literacy Achievement

A series of analyses were run to model the various posttest and follow-up data on the intervention and several other variables. Although during the pilot phase of this study (Hayden & Phillips, 2000) we found no increase in reading level as measured by CARA that could be attributed to the intervention, we did find qualitative improvements within each reading level. In the models we have run, we have found no systematic quantitative trends in the data distinguishing the control group from the intervention group. In the case of the CARA criterion measure, for example, the pretest, posttest, and follow-up scores were so highly interrelated (0.83 to 0.93) as to leave little variance to be explained once the effect of the pretest had been accounted for. The fact that we found no change in the parents' reading level brought about by the 90 hours of intervention spread over 12 weeks might be explained by their age and the assumption that adults require intensive and sustained interventions.

Qualitative Analyses

Results of the Observations

Three major themes surface from the observational data – classroom atmosphere, scaffolding, and fidelity to program rationale.

Classroom Atmosphere. Classroom atmosphere appeared to be dependent on a variety of factors – the number of individuals in the room for the size of the room, the planned activities for the day and the interrelationships between the early-years and adult only facilitators. In some instances, the room was far too small to accommodate the numbers of parents and children with the result that the noise level was distressing for many of the occupants. The crowded situation lent itself to parents raising their voices to be heard; there was not enough space to allow for several parent-child dyads to work at a centre at the same time, causing frustration on the part of the children; during circle time, parents had to sit outside the circle on chairs around the room rather than having the children close to them with the result that they became spectators of the shared events rather than participants. One parent noted to the observer that she hated the joint sessions as she felt as if she was in a "sardine can and couldn't wait for the time to be over." However, such congested conditions were the exception rather than the rule. Generally, the early-years rooms (where all of the joint sessions took place) were satisfactory and allowed for freedom of movement without difficulty. In these situations, parents had the space to work quietly with a child or find a location where they could speak in private to a child who was experiencing frustration. Most of the joint sessions, occurred within a warm and emotionally supportive environment where parent-child dyads found the space to explore the concepts of the day with pleasure and enjoyment.

Another factor that influenced classroom atmosphere was the quality and quantity of the planned activities. Generally, these activities had been previously discussed in the adult program with participants giving clear input into what they thought they might do with their children within the framework of the theme. For example, in the *Developing Language for Literacy* Unit which occurred around Halloween, parents in one program decided that they would have the children make Jack-o-Lanterns from small pumpkins, make their own treat bags, make spiders from Styrofoam cups and pipe cleaners and make Halloween "goop" from cornstarch, water and food coloring. In this instance, the quantity of activities appeared to be too much for the children with the result that parents seemed to be anxious and even frustrated in trying to get everything done. They hurried their children through these activities, and in many cases were obliged to do the tasks for the children so they could take home the completed objects. In another instance, parents decided to have the children help make a family photographic book for the *Early Reading Unit.* Several parents brought too many photographs for the children to choose from and in some cases, the children did not recognize the people in the photographs. Here again, confusion and frustration ensued and in a couple of instances, the children just left the task and went to play. Generally, however, the type and number of activities planned by the parents were most appropriate and involved the children quite well although what seemed suitable for a five-year-old child might be a daunting task for a three-year-old in the same program. One mother who was making a puppet with her three year old son commented: "It seemed like a good idea upstairs (the adult program) but I think he's just not interested or it is just too hard for him. He can't cut well so I have to do it for him."

The relationships between facilitators of the child and adult programs usually were very good. They shared leadership over how the joint sessions might evolve; they supported one another's decisions; they collaborated to resolve difficult situations; they modeled sound discipline strategies as well as appropriate approaches for encouraging risk-taking on the part of the children; they demonstrated a myriad of ways to scaffold children's learning; they worked together to develop a community of learners and demonstrated that they were just two of the learners in that community; they praised parents and children for their efforts; and when asked questions by parents, they frequently sought the advice of their teaching peer, in front of the parent, before or after responding. In short, they provided a collaborative climate that was obvious to all and supported a learning environment that was warm, accepting and constructive.

In a few instances, however, cooperative efforts by the teaching team could be described as limited at best. One of the facilitators took responsibility for everything with the result that her peer had little or no input into the day's events and often was ignored by the parents during the joint session. This lack of collaboration resulted in a more chaotic environment where one voice was master and where the concept of a community of learners was absent. Fortunately, such occurrences were rare. Generally, facilitators worked well together and with the parents; they moved through the room easily, providing assistance to both parents and children when needed but usually taking a back seat by allowing the parents to act as their children's teachers.

Scaffolding. One of the primary objectives of the *Learning Together* program was for parents to learn how to scaffold their children's learning. An examination of the adult-only program lesson plans indicate that this topic surfaced regularly and frequently became a focus for parent journal comments. In other words, parents were exposed to the importance of mediating children's learning and developing strategies to encourage joint parent-child engagement in a task. Landry and Smith (2005) contend that "maintaining attention" or "redirecting attention" (p. 139) have different results in the attainment of different verbal abilities with the former being more successful in promoting language development. In the *Learning Together* program, parents became quite skilled at noticing what their children were attending to in a task and catching that moment to build upon the child's interest with their own language input. In other words, they were instrumental in helping their children to sustain focus on a task while at the same time enhancing their opportunities to hear and use more sophisticated language. A couple of examples highlight how two different parents maintained or redirected attention.

The theme was Early Reading. Parents and children had gathered together to listen to a repetitive book, *Emily's House* (Scharer, 1993). Most of the children were snuggled in their parents' arms where they listened to and joined in the repetitive refrain of the story. Little interaction occurred between the dyads during the reading event other than smiles and laughter. Upon completion of the reading, parents and children went to a craft table where paper plates, glue, fabric, buttons, feathers, pens, crayons, and paper were available. Parents and children then proceeded to draw one of the animals from the story on the paper plate and decorate it accordingly. One father and his four-year-old daughter began a conversation as to which animal they would draw. The child finally decided on a cow. The conversation ensued as follows:

Father: How should we draw it?

Daughter: I don't know.

Father: Let's see. Remember the cows we saw on the way to Elk Island Park? What did they look like?

Daughter: They were big and got spots on them.

Father: Great! Anything else? How many legs?

Daughter: I want buttons for the spots.

Father: Good for you. How many legs? Two, four?

Daughter: Four and long, long tails.

Father: Yeah! Right! See, you remember. Anything else? Like the color?

Daughter: I think black – no, black and white. Now draw the cow, Dad.

Father : OK – big and black and white and spots and four legs and a tail. I think you could draw it. Here's the pencil.

The child picked up the pencil and began to draw a round shape in the centre of the paper plate. The father leaned towards her and offered supportive comments such as "Great," "You got it." "Now for the legs." "This is really good." The child completed her drawing.

Father: Now what do we do?

Daughter: Color it and put the buttons on.

   She reaches for the glue.

Father: Buttons first? OK. You want those ones? Why?

Daughter: They're big and the cow is big too.

The child continued working on her cow image; parent and child continued chatting in the same manner, building upon one another's comments.

As this example demonstrates, the parent sustained the child's interest in the task by relating her choice of animal to one she had seen on a family outing, by suggesting elements she might put in her drawing, by accepting her lead as to how she might complete her work, by inserting questions and comments to keep the conversation going, and by recognizing the child's efforts. At no time did the child indicate she wished to move away from the task. Rather, her father's behavior assisted her in maintaining interest in what she was doing.

When we compare this dyad's conversation with another where the parent did not attempt to maintain the child's interest in what is occurring but rather redirected attention elsewhere when the child's interest waned. A mother and four-year-old son were together at the craft table where the activity of the day was to engage the children to use felt pens to paint faces and hair on 10 Popsicle sticks. This activity was connected to the Writing and Drawing theme and related to the rhyme, *Ten Little Monkeys Sleeping in a Bed* which the children had sung earlier in the day. The notation "There was one in the bed and the little one said "Roll Over" had been written on strips of paper for pasting on the construction paper bed when the drawing of the faces was finished.

Mother: OK now, we have to count out ten sticks.

Son: One, two, three, four. You do it Mom.

Mother: OK – five, six, seven, eight, nine, ten. There you are. Now you have to paint faces and hair on all of them and when they're all done we can put them in the paper bed.

The child picks up a felt pen and starts to draw a face. He makes two large eyes and a nose.

Child: No room for the hair.

Mother: Just leave it; do another one.

Again the child starts to draw but is not any more successful than his first attempt. He looks around the room. He picks another stick and draws lines at the top.

Child: I want to play.

Mother: Just do a few more, then you can play.

The child picks another stick and "scribbles" all over it.

Mother: You can do better than that. Maybe you'd better go play.

As this example demonstrates, there was limited interaction between parent and child. Once the child felt he was not successful, the parent did not attempt to scaffold his learning. Rather, she remained somewhat aloof from the activity; she did not make suggestions as to how he might do the task, nor did she demonstrate for him what was expected of him. The mother's language did not encourage the child to continue. She was more directive than cooperative in offering assistance. Frustration followed with the result that she sanctioned his leaving the activity to go play.

It may not be fair to judge a parent on a one time observation because a myriad of factors could have influenced her behavior – not feeling well, being distracted by a family problem, etc. Although there were other incidences of parents not scaffolding behaviors, in the majority of situations observed, parents mediated their children's learning in very effective ways. They encouraged their children to explore; they engaged them in conversations; they were sensitive to their children's needs and frequently followed the children's lead in how a task should be done. They assisted when necessary, giving them ideas to extend an activity; they involved their children in the joint reading time using appropriate strategies such as pointing out objects in a book's pictures, highlighting letters the child might know, asking questions and encouraging the children to tell them what they liked best about a story. Their non-verbal behaviors demonstrated warmth and encouragement that enticed the children to persist with a task. They were obviously pleased with their children's efforts and delighted in their development. As one parent noted: "My son is learning so much in this program; I am just amazed. We both just love coming here."

Scaffolding also was observed across parents and children as they played and worked with their children. It was not unusual for a parent to assist another parent's child or to give suggestions to another parent on how a task might be made easier for a youngster. These suggestions took place, by and large, during play or directed activity times where several parent-child dyads were in proximity. A conversation between a parent and child often overflowed to another parent-child couple who then, in turn, wove their conversation to include the other pair. There was a sense that many of the adults felt that they could contribute to the learning of any child, not just their own. They collaborated in maintaining the children on task; they encouraged one another's children in what they were doing; and they also often made positive reference when they saw a peer simplifying or extending a task for the child. In other words, there appeared to be a strong learning community within most program sites.

There were some parents, in a few of the programs, who elected to work alone with their children. They chose locations away from others even to the extent of moving craft materials to their chosen space rather than to take a place at a central table with peers. A few sat off to the side during circle time. Their reasons for their conduct varied. One mother commented that she found it easier to play and work with her daughter when there were fewer distractions. Another pointed out that this joint session time was the only time she had alone with her child because so many people lived in her house. A few of the ESL parents mentioned that their English was not good enough and they preferred to speak their home language with their children during the craft or play times. None of these parents indicated that they felt isolated or unwanted by the group.

It should also be noted that the facilitators also scaffolded the children's learning during the joint sessions. Their attention to whom might be having difficulty, their awareness of when parents struggled to maintain their children's interest in a task, their gentle encouragement of both parents and children, and their sensitivity to stepping in or stepping away when the occasion demanded was clear evidence of their knowledge of appropriate teaching strategies for both adults and children. They encouraged parents to take charge but were there with support when required.

Opportunities to witness many different events within the adult session occurred on numerous occasions. On these occasions, it was noted that some adults were less engaged in reading and writing text. With respect to reading, the facilitator brought to the attention of the adults particular reading strategies such as making predictions, using context clues to determine unknown words, and generating background knowledge. The facilitator seemed to be of the understanding that adults could use these strategies for their own reading benefit as well as when they read to their children. However, when the adults were presented with text to read, many of them did not appear to transfer the use of these strategies to the reading task at hand.

One example highlights this point quite clearly. Through discussion, the adults generated a comprehensive list of words and phrases in response to the facilitator asking them to tell her all they knew about cooking. She wrote their comments on chart paper. After this brainstorming episode, the facilitator then gave them a short piece of text to read about cooking and noted that they would discuss the article after they had read it. The author of the article presented a humorous point of view of the frustrations of cooking for her family as the only time they congratulated her for her culinary efforts was when she ordered food from local fast food outlets. In observing the group, it became apparent that some of the participants did not see the humor in the article even though the group had expressed similar points of view during the brainstorming. Two women, in particular, noted that "it (the article) was boring" and did not attempt to finish it. They chatted quietly while their peers continued to read. The ensuing discussion highlighted the fact that most of the group saw clear connections between their views of cooking and those of the author. One mother even noted that "the writer used some of our words like "tedious," "tiresome" and "a thankless job."

The gap between the facilitator highlighting or modeling a strategy and some of the parents' failure to use the strategy in their reading in class was observed. It seems that many of the adults already had used the strategy successfully prior to program participation and that the discussion or modeling of the strategy served only as reinforcement. For others who distanced themselves from the class readings, it seems that their understanding of when and where to use the strategy was not sufficiently clear to use independently. In such cases, facilitators need to be more aware of the difficulties some of their participants may have and work more individually with them to ensure greater appreciation and understanding of the strategy.

Parental interest in writing was observed to be more personal rather than in response to a task set by the facilitator. Although many of the parents wrote comments about their interactions with their children during the joint sessions, some of these writings were extended during the adult-only sessions. However, they preferred to compose for their own purposes and enjoyment. Several parents remarked that they were keeping a journal. One woman remarked that the Learning Together program had "set her on the path to keeping a family history" with her journal. She noted that she "wrote in it once a week, just a sort of diary of the family happenings so that one day the children could see all the things they did together as a family." She was extremely enthused by her efforts and said that her husband "really likes to read it." Other parents spoke of writing birth stories of their children and some noted they were writing poetry. One woman mentioned that when someone gave her a recipe, she carefully copied it into a "special recipe book" that she hoped one day to pass on to her daughter.

This interest in writing was evident in most of the programs at all five sites. A few adults remarked to the researcher during sessions that they were not good spellers. They wrote because they wanted to and were given the opportunity in class to do so. Given the difficulty of finding time to write when one has the responsibility of a young family, it appears that the writing period within the program allowed parents to build confidence in their own abilities as writers. Over the course of the *Learning Together* program, it was clear that the length of their writings increased.

Fidelity to Program Information. One of the goals of the program was to help parents help their children develop as language users and as readers and writers. The curriculum was designed to meet that purpose. Observations of the joint sessions indicated that this objective was met to a considerable degree.

It was obvious that, for the most part, parents were put in charge of how the joint sessions might evolve. That is not to say that the facilitators did not plan what should be included in a session; on the contrary, they were very aware of the thematic structure of the program. They arranged and prepared for the materials (books, rhymes, craft supplies) to be available when required. In addition, they encouraged the parents to provide many of the materials such as toilet paper rolls, egg cups, fabric pieces, etc. that would enhance the children's learning. With respect to the parents' involvement, however, they were responsible for and given control over what activities might best meet their children's needs. At times, this control led to more activity than the children could handle in the time allotted as noted above, but that in itself became an adult learning situation that allowed for further discussion of children's learning within the adult-only program.

Parents also frequently took over the facilitator's position as leader during circle time. They often brought their own children's books from home to read to the group; they suggested rhymes and games that the children could play; and they helped organize field trips. On one occasion, a parent took it upon herself to walk around the neighborhood and identify the environmental print located there. She subsequently borrowed a camera from a friend and took pictures of this print which she showed to the children before their environmental print walk. Another parent went to a local print store and asked if she could have the paper from the recycle bin which she then distributed to all the parents for home drawing and writing episodes. Such initiatives on the part of parents were not unusual.

Parents were also encouraged to observe their children both during the joint sessions and at home so that they could determine how their children were progressing. Many of them shared stories during snack time of what they had seen their children doing and what they were learning about their children's development. They delighted in their children's advancement and they appeared pleased at their own confidence in being able to identify this growth. One parent mentioned that she "never knew you could know so much about kids; it's not just stuff about how to keep them healthy but to watch them grow and learn and know what they are learning." Such a view was prevalent among many of the parents.

The curriculum was implemented well with continual focus on encouraging what was best for the young children's language and literacy development. The early-years classrooms were well equipped with resources designed to meet that end. Different centres such as house, block, dress-up, listening, painting and drawing, together with centres designed to meet the thematic units were found in all program sites. In addition, a copious supply of literacy materials such as books, magazines, different kinds of paper and writing tools, together with literacy materials more usually found in the home such as flyers, "junk mail," recipe books, etc., were placed at various locations around the room. In other words, the children had the opportunity to be immersed in print and had access to these print materials not only for their joint parent activities but also for their own play activities during the sessions where parents were not present. A computer was also available in some of the locations where the children worked through different programs appropriate for their ages. Children's art work and their attempts at writing were clearly displayed around the room. The children's name tags were often used by the early-years facilitator to talk about different letters of the alphabet. Signs, indicating the different centres, were posted around the rooms which were also used for letter recognition.

Oral language games, rhymes, finger plays, and oral storytelling supplemented the usual verbal exchanges between facilitators and children. The joint activities encouraged parent-child oral language interactions as did the inclusion of special guest speakers such as a nurse, a veterinarian, or a policeman who spoke to the children on their areas of expertise. The listening centre was one of the children's favorites where they could listen to songs or recorded books, many of which had been read several times previously during circle time.

The program, therefore, could best be described as an excellent opportunity to put into practice all of the elements of a sound early intervention program that included parents as integral to its success. The kinds of activities provided for the children were, for the most part, suitable for their age ranges. Opportunities to play, listen, talk, share experiences, read and write were numerous. Literacy was woven into the fabric of the activities in very casual and incidental ways but intentionally so. One might say that the children were learning why and how literacy is used in the world.

Results of the Interviews

The first major section reports data analysis for the treatment participants for whom we have full interview data, that is pretest, posttest, first follow-up, second follow-up, and third follow-up interviews. Due to insufficient numbers of children and parents remaining in the program for quantitative analyses, fourth follow-up data are not discussed.

Fourteen *Learning Together* programs were conducted over a period of 19 months, four of which were offered in rural areas. Participation varied from four to ten parents across program sites. Interviews were conducted with parents prior to program intervention, at the conclusion of the program participation, and subsequently on program conclusion anniversary dates for the next three years. Parents were given an honorarium of $100 for each of the three final interviews. While the total number of parents enrolled in the *Learning Together* program totaled 147, the number of participants on which complete interview data were collected was 47. This is a significant number given the length of the study (three years after program participation) and the transient nature of the population under investigation.

Research assistants, trained by the researchers, conducted individual interviews with program parents. All assistants had obtained at least an undergraduate degree and several held graduate degrees. Training for the data collection during interviews focused the research assistants' attention on supporting parents to expand their responses to individual questions. In some instances, the same research assistant was available to conduct all interviews with the same participants over the four-year period. When such instances occurred, a considerable measure of trust occurred between the assistant and the participating parent, thereby allowing for greater depth and breadth of data collection. In other cases, different interviewers met with parents across the data collection period. Interviews took place in participants' homes, the program sites (schools), local restaurants, motels, or community libraries. Where interviews were conducted reflected participant choice. The interviewers made notes during their discussions with parents, expanded on these notes later, and also wrote anecdotal reports concerning observations they made or information given to them that had not been directly focused on particular questions.

Reasons for Enrolling in Program. Of the 47 parents for whom we have full three-year data following program intervention, 68% professed that their reason for enrolling in the program was to help their children succeed in school. As one parent mentioned, "I think this program will give my child a good start. His older brother has not had an easy time learning to read – most of us in this family are not good readers so this may be a chance to give him a leg up." Another parent commented that she had "heard somewhere that parents can help their kids get ready to read before they go to school and this program seems to be a good way to do that."

Other reasons for participation in *Learning Together* centred upon the more social aspects of the program. "It'll be a chance to be with other adults," commented one mother. "Why wouldn't you go?" said another parent. "It's *free* (her emphasis). They even provide babysitting for your little ones. Your kid gets a chance to learn things, meet with other kids and the parents can get together as well. Sounds wonderful to me." Comments such as "a chance to get out of the house a couple of times a week," "meeting other moms," "improve my English" and "get to know other people" were not unusual. The fact that the program would not be any financial burden was mentioned by close to 50% of the parents.

Generally, however, parents were very unsure as to what they might learn. Such uncertainty is perhaps not unusual given that they had only a broad view of the program's content. This overview had been presented at a "taster session" a couple of weeks prior to program initiation. Approximately 17% mentioned they hoped to improve their own literacy abilities and of that percentage, the majority were second language learners.

Throughout the interviews, there was an atmosphere of hope and positive anticipation that the program would be beneficial to the children, and in part to the adults themselves. Despite difficult financial, social and emotional challenges, those who elected to participate in the program considered their enrollment to be a step in the right direction for improving their circumstances.

Adults' Early Home Experiences. Several of the parents shared memories of their experiences of growing up although the interviewers did not directly ask for this information. Of those who did (50%), the majority (60%) spoke warmly of that period in their lives. "My mother was a wonder," remarked one mother. "How she managed so well with eight of us is a miracle. She rarely lost her patience and money was a problem all the time. But she laughed a lot." Another noted, "We lived with my grandparents. My grandma was always cooking and I can still remember the smell of cinnamon buns. It was a happy house." One father explained how his father would take him hunting in the fall and the celebrations they had when they came home with a moose. "We ate like kings," he remarked.

These adults spoke warmly of their early lives, of being "comfortable," "happy" and "supported by loving parents."

For some of the adults, however, growing up was a time of struggle. "My father committed suicide when I was six," reported one participant, "and then my mother did the same when I was ten." This woman recounted how she was "shuttled off to relatives" as were some of her siblings, an event that resulted in her acting as "unpaid babysitter" for various cousins. "Often I couldn't go to school because I had to look after the baby," she commented. To add fuel to her unfortunate circumstances, she noted that her uncle beat her about the head if she complained with the result that she learned early in life "not to make waves." When she was fifteen, she ran away from this environment, worked on the streets for a few years during which time she lived with a fellow who also beat her when he drank, which was frequently. "My father hit everyone when he drank," commented another parent. "When we saw him coming, we used to run out the back door. He beat my mother a lot and even my youngest brother who was only about two and couldn't stop crying. That's when my mom took us away."

Family discussions often evolved into heated arguments, which in turn resulted in family members shouting derogatory comments at one another. "My mother was always picking on me, telling me I would amount to nothing," said one participant. I left home at sixteen – couldn't take it anymore." "No one ever told me they loved me," reported another woman. "It was always talk about what was wrong with me; I felt that if I wasn't there, things would be OK."

Poverty was often the source of difficulty during these formative years. "We were always moving," stated a mother. "My dad would lose his job and we'd fall behind in the rent, so we had to move. And that meant I had to go to a different school. Not fun trying to fit in." Another participant commented that she often felt hungry as a child. One mother pointed out, "There never seemed to be enough money to go around. We had to make do. It wasn't so bad when I was a kid, but as a teenager, I remember feeling ashamed that I couldn't look like and be like the others in school. So I dropped out."

Adults' Own School Experiences. Many parents spoke at length about their own school experiences. Thirty-four percent reported that school had not been a problem for them. Even though many of these parents left school prior to high school graduation, they were of the opinion that family or personal circumstances rather than difficulties at school caused their early departure from academic pursuits. One mother captured the thoughts of many of her peers when she said, "I did okay in school, not the top of the class or anything, but okay. But then my dad committed suicide and things fell apart at home. My mom was drinking and I couldn't take the heat any more. So I left. That was at the beginning of Grade 10. I eventually got my GED but that was much later." Some spoke of teachers who were "good listeners," or "easy to talk to," others commented on the friends they made during their school years. Several parents noted something similar to the parent who said, "It was my fault I didn't do well in school; I was lazy." One mother noted that she "got boy crazy in Grade 8" and that "was the beginning of the end" for her. "I became pregnant in Grade 9," said another mother. "I only did it once and got pregnant. Going to school in a small town and being pregnant was not on so I had to quit."

For the majority of parents, however, school had not been a fond memory. "I hated it from about grade 4," said one mother. "I was always being teased and even bullied sometimes 'cause I was the only Aboriginal in the class. It was awful and the teachers did nothing to stop it." One woman recounted that in Junior High kids teased her unmercifully because of the clothes she wore. Another woman reported how the teacher told her, in front of the whole class that she was "dumb" and would "never learn." "Only the smart kids got attention from the teacher," remarked another mother. "I was always told 'Just do it' and I couldn't 'cause I didn't understand what to do. I felt so *stupid*" (her emphasis). Another participant reported "no matter how hard I tried at school, no one ever said I did a good job so I gave up trying and just sat there all day." Several participants commented that school was not a "good" or "fun" place to be. One woman even noted, "I wouldn't wish school on my worst enemy. It's an awful place. The kids are rotten if you are not in their club and the teachers don't care. At least that is what it was like for me. I just hope it will be better for my kids."

Even though these remarks indicate that memories about school for many participants could best be described as miserable, most parents recognized the importance of education and were hopeful that their children would succeed in academic life. They wanted their children to have opportunities to thrive in the school environment. As one parent put it so succinctly, "I want my child to be able to hold his head up, to learn and grow to be good at whatever he chooses to do." Enrollment in the *Learning Together* program served as a bridge to that success in their opinion, and would help them as adults learn how to help their children.

Literacy Activities in the Home. Twenty-six percent of parents indicated they made use of the library either occasionally or frequently. The majority of these parents lived in the urban areas. One parent noted, "The library is great. We go every Saturday to get books and videos." These parents reported reading to their children either several times a week or on a daily basis. They were aware of their children's favorite books. Most of these families had some children's books in the home although the number was small. "It's too expensive to buy books," said one mother, "so we go to the library to get them."

The parents encouraged their children's play with literacy, involved them in trying to write their names and helped with writing birthday cards; they played games with them, and they watched TV together. Most of these parents also considered that children learn to read by being read to and by talking about words and letters. Generally, these parents integrated literacy into the routines of daily life without consciously being aware of what their children were learning from them or even that they were learning anything important for their literacy development.

Religious texts were a major source of print for many of the parents themselves. Several diligently read the Bible each day, and told Bible stories to their children. One mother even kept a reflective journal of her thoughts about her Bible reading. "I read the Bible every day," said one father. "I sometimes even read it aloud to the kids but it's hard for them to understand it." The 33% of parents who used religious texts came primarily from the rural areas.

Over 70% of parents, however, read only occasionally to their children and made little or no use of the library. "We don't go now 'cause the kids tore books and then we had to pay," commented one parent. Although they often sang songs or told stories to their children from time to time, most parents did not indicate that they involved their children in literacy tasks such as helping them write their names, deliberately pointing out print in the environment, or sharing books at bedtime. "It's really busy in our house," commented one mother. "Getting them to bed at the end of the day is a chore and I'm exhausted by then so I never think of reading to them." Others reported similar experiences. One mother noted that she had tried a few times to read to her three-year-old child but that he never sat still and listened so she gave up the practice. "Perhaps he will be better when he is older," she said. They also were of the opinion that children learn to read mostly when they go to school.

It should be noted, however, that nearly all of the parents interacted in positive ways with their children. Many talked of going to the park to play or to have a picnic; others mentioned that they took advantage of community activities such as family swim times or skating. Several references were made to large family get-togethers where the children and their cousins had opportunities to play. There was a genuine sense, from most of the interviews, that the adults, although at times overwhelmed by the responsibility of raising their children, liked them and enjoyed being with them.

Summary

The initial interviews provided a broad picture of the family contexts for the participants. The 47 adults were generous in sharing information about their own learning experiences and their expectations for the program. While the majority focused on the benefits that would accrue to their children as a result of participation, some participants noted that they too would profit from the experience. The minority reported good memories of their own school experiences; for the majority of participants this time in their lives had been quite problematic. Early school leaving was generally a result of personal (e.g. pregnancy) or family circumstances (e.g., moving location, job loss, illness). The majority did not make use of the library and in general read only infrequently to their children. Most participants were of the opinion that children learned to read in school. Overall, parents were hopeful for their children and considered that the *Learning Together* program would help them to get a good start on their academic careers. Despite financial, social and emotional difficulties, the parents were providing loving and supportive home environments for their children and were genuinely excited about this new journey together.

Post-Program Interviews

After the completion of the program, participants were interviewed again. The focus for this interview was their judgments about the program and the effect it may have had on them, their children and the whole family.

General Response to the Program. Overall, parents reported being very pleased with the program. Over 90% indicated that they enjoyed it and found it interesting. Furthermore, 80% found the content of the program, the readings and handouts provided by the facilitators as interesting, new, motivating, and exciting. The fact that many of the participants commented that the program allowed them to "make new friends," "be with other adults for part of the routine week," "have time with other adults to talk about kids growing up" and "socialize" as the most interesting part of the program appears to indicate that the program helped to mitigate social isolation and loneliness.

Several parents indicated their surprise at their own learning. "I didn't expect to learn much for myself," said one participant. "I came for my kid. But I learned a lot too and that made it all so interesting for me. Not just about reading and writing, but about parenting and child development." Other parents echoed this view quite frequently. One mother commented that the program had "helped her become a better reader. I am more aware of what I am reading. I am able to comprehend and remember details found in the reading. My writing has got better too." Another noted that her "writing has improved a lot 'cause of brainstorming her ideas first." Although this parent recognized that she still had "trouble editing," she "was getting better at it." One mother commented, "My reading has helped my writing. When I am upset, I write my thoughts out and now I actually read those thoughts afterwards."

Some participants considered their children's development as "the best part of the program." "It was great seeing how she was learning," said one mother. "Each day brought something new along." "Another noted that her child had "become obsessed with letters and words," which she felt "would not have happened without the program. So, it was great." One father indicated that learning "how to get literacy into everyday play" was the most appealing aspect of the program for him. "It's quite simple really when you think of it, but no one ever told me what to do before."

Other parents considered the fact that both parent and child went to the program together as the most interesting aspect. "We used to get ready each day together. It was like an outing for us, together," commented one parent. "It's not often you get to do things together," said another. "Well, we really weren't together that much, but we went together and came home together and we both had things to tell Dad." One may assume that such views reflect a strengthening parent-child relationship.

Seventy percent of participants noted they attended most sessions; those that they missed were for genuine reasons – their own or their children's illness, job interviews, inclement weather, or some unforeseen condition such as having to wait for a plumber to fix a broken toilet. Although the "novelty of the program" wore off after the first month or so, as noted by one parent, the children "insisted on going" so "it would have been difficult to skip." Such a comment shows the influence the children may have on adult participation.

Rating of Learning Together Program

Adult Component. Seventy-eight percent of participants considered the adult component of the program "worthwhile," "a great learning experience," "very satisfactory," or "excellent." On a scale of 1 to 10, most of these parents rated it either a nine or ten. When asked their reasons for such ratings, several indicated that the sensitivity of the facilitator allowed them to feel secure in asking questions or making comments about the content of the program or a particular subject under discussion. "After the first couple of times I felt really comfortable there. Like everyone in the room was friendly and we shared ideas," commented one participant. "The program was just super. We learned so much about how kids learn, about how we can help them," noted one mother. Another parent noted, "We discussed all sorts of things: discipline, how to get kids to eat proper food, and good ways to read books to kids. I didn't think I would get much out of it, but I did." One mother responded by saying, "The topics were really interesting and I really liked preparing things to do with the kids. It was awesome." One parent liked the fact that the program was structured so that what the adults "were doing related to what the kids were doing."

Other comments focused on the camaraderie that developed among those participating. A participant remarked, "We became good friends and I know lots of us will keep in touch. One mom has already set up a meeting in her house for next month." "I just loved being with other adults," commented another. "There were four of us in our group so we got to know one another very well and shared a lot of ideas. I learned a lot from them," remarked another parent. It was a bit like a social club, good people together. Oh, sure we were learning stuff, but I thought the social aspect was the best." Regarding their own reading improvement, several participants reported that the tips they got on how to improve were really helpful. "I'm not a good reader," noted one mother. "But the teacher showed us things to do to help – like thinking about what we know about a subject before we read about it, or looking at pictures for hints. That was so helpful." Another mother agreed when she remarked that her own reading had "really improved" with the result that she felt more comfortable reading magazines and newspapers as a result of her participation in the program.

Many parents suggested that the length of the program was too short. "It should go all year," commented one mother. "There is so much to learn and the kids really benefit from being with the other kids in the kids' part." A father reflected that he "really missed going to the program once it was over" with his son. "It was a special time for me, for him, for both of us. I would go with him again in a minute if I could." Other participants were of a similar opinion. One mother considered the length of each session "just right for me and my daughter" but that "overall, I would have liked it [the program] to go on longer – like all year. She was learning so much about reading and writing and counting and her colors and things." "I think it would have been best to go longer – like 20 weeks or so," commented another parent. "I felt things were a bit rushed, like we would've had more time to talk and things."

While the majority viewed the programs very positively, approximately 20% of the participants suggested some revisions. One parent said, "There should be more of a focus on conventions and learning how to write. I have trouble with big words and would like to have seen more reading strategies for adults." Another parent believed that "there were so many topics to cover that I think the program should have gone all year round. At times, we seemed rushed, especially when we had crafts to do." Some parents also thought that there didn't seem to be enough attention paid to helping them become better readers. "Somehow I thought my own reading would improve, but I don't think it did even though we talked quite a bit about comprehension," remarked a mother.

Generally the participants viewed the adult component of the program very positively. It appeared to meet their needs and they enjoyed their time. The facilitators' warmth and understanding, the opportunity to build relationships and share ideas with other adults together with the content of the course appeared to be sufficiently comprehensive to engage them.

Child Component. Like the adult component of the program, parents considered the child component very positively with over 80% giving it a rating of eight, nine or ten. Comments such as "excellent," "wonderful," "a great learning experience for kids," "all kids should have the chance of being in a program like this," and "he just loved it and cried the day he was sick and couldn't go," were frequent. Most parents thought the children learned a lot about books, about letters and words, about coloring and printing, and how to get along with other children. This latter feature was noted in numerous interviews. One may presume, therefore, that the social aspect of learning was important to the parents, a mirror of their own focus on the social response within their own program component.

Parents were enthusiastic in their praise for the child component facilitators and aides. "They were wonderful," commented one parent. "They really got the children involved even when they were reluctant to do so." Another mother remarked, "I was in awe of how much the kids did each day. It was great to hear him tell his dad about his time there." Another commented, "It was amazing. Great room with so many things for the kids to do and learn from." A parent recounted how one day her child told her "all about the book the teacher had read and how he wanted her [his mother] to get the book so she could read it to him again." One mother remarked that she thought the facilitators were very "skilled at getting the kids involved" and "that they had so much for the kids to do that no one could get bored."

While few parents commented on the actual content of the child component, there appeared to be a general feeling that the children were learning a great deal during their time in the program. Comments such as "She's learned to print her name," "He knows all his colors now," "She wants me to read to her now," "She looks at all the words and letters when we go for a walk," and "He sings rhymes and songs so easily now," give an indication that parents recognized their children's growth in language and literacy. In short, parents considered the child component of the program a valuable learning experience for their children.

Joint Sessions. Parental response was less positive for the joint sessions than for the other two program components. Just over 60% of participants rated this feature of the program within an 8-10 rating. For those who considered it a constructive element, comments generally focused on the opportunity for parents to put into practice what they had discussed and learned in the adult section of the program. "I loved how we prepared what to do when we met with the children," said one mother, "and then got the chance to do it right away with them in their own classroom." Another remarked, "I'm glad we had the get-together with the kids. We had real fun together and we could practice what we learned." Others noted that "being in the children's classroom was important 'cause we could see what the kids were doing," "We could see how our kids interacted with other kids," "I could talk with him about the things in the classroom," and "It was something me and my child looked forward to, being together." One mother noted that "it was the highlight of the whole program" for her. "I loved going down to her room; she looked forward to my coming and then we did things together before going home. It was great." Another parent remarked, "Doing the crafts and field trips together was super." Such comments are representative of many of the participants.

Other parents, however, were less complimentary. They thought things were quite disorganized during the joint sessions; they grumbled about the "lack of space for so many people in one small room"; they considered that some parents "didn't really interact with their children" or "completed the task on their own while their children watched"; they commented upon the fact that often it was "not clear which facilitator was in charge" of the joint events. Several felt that the joint sessions were a "total waste of time" and that "it would have been better just "to stay in separate programs."

Such views, while prevalent, need to be taken in context, however. Most of these comments surfaced in the first few programs offered, during what one might term the growing pains of the program. Based on facilitator surveys at the conclusion of these initial programs, revisions were made to find more appropriate site locations, and to improve preparation of the facilitators for the joint sessions. While not all criticisms disappeared during subsequent program offerings, better procedures were generally put in place to ensure greater parent-child interactions during these shared experiences.

Effect of Program on Home Literacy Activities

Parents were very vocal in their discussions of how the program had influenced their home literacy activities. Over 80% indicated that home literacy activities were more frequent and more varied, and that they were much more aware of how they could weave literacy into the daily routines of family life. For example, 74% mentioned that they were more frequent library users, with many of them noting that they went to this community service a couple of times a month. Perhaps even more important, 90% indicated that they were reading to their children at least once a day. In addition, the quality of the shared readings had changed dramatically. "I used to read to my kid,'" said one parent. "But now, I really read to her. We talk about the book before we read it by looking at the front cover; I let her talk so much more as well and point things out to her." Another parent said that before she hated reading the same book over to her child but that now she knew how important rereading books was and so she was much more likely to do so. "My daughter loves being read to now," she noted.

Other parents talked about the strategies they had learned in the program that would engage their children with books. "She picks out her own books now at the library," commented one parent. Others referred to tracking the print with their finger when they read with the child, looking at the pictures for clues to the story, showing the child where they were reading, talking about the book, letting the child turn the pages of the book, connecting the book's characters or content to the child's life, encouraging the child to ask questions or make comments during the reading, or pausing so that the child could predict the next part of the text when the book was of a predictable nature. Use of these strategies came about as a result of program participation. As one mother noted, "I never knew before you could do so much to get a kid involved in a story reading." Another remarked that "reading together is so much more fun now. She [her daughter] really gets involved. She wants me to read the book over and over."

Interestingly, many of the parents mentioned the concept of their modeling of reading. One mother noted, "I've learned to be a good role model. When I read, she now goes to get her book and she sits beside me turning her pages and talking about the pictures." Other participants revealed that they made a point of reading when their children were around. Such reading consisted of newspapers, magazines, flyers, and books. "I'll look through the flyers," commented one mother, "while she is sitting on my lap and we'll talk about what we should get at the store. She watches me write out the grocery list which I never did before and sometimes she scribbles her list too."

Parents commented upon how they involved their children more frequently in literacy events such as writing their own birthday invitations, Christmas cards, or wish lists for Santa Claus, attending to environmental print or making use of the print that comes into the home such as letters, magazines or flyers. "I let him make his own cards, now," said a mother. "Before, I thought he was too small to do those things – he's only 3½ - but he loves doing it." One mother reflected that when she was sorting out winter clothing into boxes for storage, she encouraged her child to label the containers. "He copied what I wrote down for him and did a good job of it." Another parent acknowledged how much the section on environmental print had influenced her behavior. "I really pay attention to the print around us," she remarked. "This was a real eye-opener for me. I get her to pick things out of the cupboard for supper and have her tell me how she knows what they are. The same when we go for a drive. It's amazing how much she knows." One father commented that he was much more vocal with his child about why and how he uses print. "I tell him why I am looking in the TV Guide – about looking for the time and what station," he noted. Such engagement of children in home literacy events permeated their conversations and reflected efforts by the adults to highlight the functions of print for their children.

Participants also noted that they had a greater range of literacy materials available for their children. These resources included coloring books, paper, pencils, crayons and paint, and a larger selection of children's books, most of which were available to the children who had been in the program. They also gave the children greater access to the "adult" print found in the home such as magazines, grocery flyers, junk mail, and recipe books. "She cuts and pastes things from the flyers before we go to the store," observed one mother. Within the same context, another parent commented that her four-year-old was interested in copying out the words she wrote down for her grocery list and then crossing them off when they found them in the store. A mother claimed that she now requests family members buy books as gifts for birthdays and Christmas so that her children will have a larger collection of their own. Another parent indicated that she had gone to an office supply store and asked for the discarded paper destined for the recycle bin. "They gave me a huge load of paper so the kids have lots of paper to draw and write on. And we've made a corner of the kitchen to show off their work. It's great," she noted. The greater accessibility to print materials together with the parents' encouragement of their use and praise for so doing lured the children to greater experimentation with print during their preschool years.

Several parents commented on the fact that they had "designed" a location in the home where the child could easily access print materials or use the print materials without asking for assistance. A mother recounted that her husband had repainted an old TV table in bright colors. "This is where she keeps all her writing stuff," she noted. "She calls it her desk and she gets upset if the other children go there." Another mother recounted that they used to keep the children's books up high so that they would not get damaged. "Now she has several right beside her bed on a shelf. She often pulls one out and reads to herself or her dolls," reported this mother. One mother described how she had bought a pencil sharpener for her four-year-old child who spent a whole day sharpening six pencils until they just became stubs. "But when I got her new ones, I explained that she could only sharpen them when they needed it or I would have to put it away where she couldn't get it. She never did it again. So I guess the novelty wore off and now her sharpener is in her pencil box."

Summary

Generally, the participants rated the program highly both from their own experiences and those of their children. More than 90% indicated they would recommend the program to others. The parents' own literacy abilities, in their opinions, improved. They were more confident of their own abilities as readers and writers and more secure in their abilities to help their children on their literacy journey. They were reading and writing more often and were making efforts to make sure their children saw them engaged in these activities. In addition, they believed their children had learned a great deal not only from a social perspective but also about reading and writing. They also contended that the children increased their knowledge about print because their parents were making print materials more varied and more accessible in the home. They were encouraging child participation in home literacy events on a more conscious level and were impressed by the children's involvement and development. In short, most parents reported putting into practice much of what they learned in the program without too much difficulty and were very positive about the results of those efforts to highlight literacy in the home.

First Follow-Up Interview

This interview took place approximately one year after program participation. Changes had occurred in the lives of some families over this period of time. Some had moved to a new location, either within the area in which they previously lived or further away to a reservation. Six families welcomed a new baby and were coping with the stress of the new family addition. In some families, the fathers had lost their jobs with the result that the participating mothers had to go to work full-or part-time to meet the families' financial responsibilities. One mother had lost her children to government care for a period of four months as a result of her spending time in an alcoholic rehabilitation centre. Generally, however, the families who participated in the program maintained their usual routines taking into account their children's increased literacy. Some children were enrolled in preschool, and others had started kindergarten and even grade one.

Over 80% of the parents commented that they often thought back to the program. "I wish it were still going on," said one mother. "I often think about the things we did in the program and the good time I had with the other women," remarked another. One parent noted, "I look over my book about once a month to help me remember some of the things I learned." She was referring to the binder of handouts and activities that each parent collected and used during the program. Another parent echoed this view when she stated, "The binder is a bit of a bible for me. If I think I should do other things with my kid, I go through it and get ideas in it." "I hope they have the program again when my baby is old enough to go," observed another mother. "Now that I know something, I could really help her when she is old enough." Reflections such as these were frequent among the parents and indicate, to some degree, that the program continued to have an influence on their lives.

When asked what kinds of activities the adults and the children performed over the past year, the list they provided was comprehensive: singing songs; telling stories; reading stories; playing "I Spy" for objects or words when driving in the car; writing shopping lists, birthday cards and notes; discussing TV shows; playing games; and using the computer. In addition, nearly 70% reported making use of the library quite frequently – once or twice a month. Bedtime reading was mentioned by 63% of participants. "There's no way we would get away without reading to her every night," commented one mother. "She'd have a hissy fit if we did."

Continued Influence of Program on Home Literacy Activities. Approximately 56% of parents had the opinion that their participation in the program had influenced the quality of their home literacy activities. One mother recounted how her four-year-old son often wrote letters in the snow or made them with twigs. "I don't think I would have paid much attention to that if I hadn't been in the program. Maybe he wouldn't even have tried to write letters. I don't know. But the program taught me the importance of that writing so I always congratulate him and encourage him." Another parent mentioned how her daughter often asked about words in a book they read together. "She's older now so I suppose it is natural to ask about words but I think the way I read with her has helped her focus more on the words," commented this mother.

Perhaps most interesting was the parents' responses to the children's early attempts to read and write. They noted that their children were able to write their own names, make lists, read to pets and dolls, had memorized the text of shared books, made labels for objects, pointed out letters in the community and the home, asked about words and letters, often asked visitors or other family members to read to them, or showed them the drawings and writings they had done. As one mother put it, "There is a lot more going on in our house with reading and writing. We might've been doing it without the program but I don't think we would have appreciated it as much – their learning about reading and writing, I mean. So I pick on those things better, I think 'cause now I know they are important."

For some parents, the question of how the program continued to be an influence on home literacy activities received little response. "I don't know," commented one mother. "We just continue to do our own thing." Another remarked that she thought the program had little effect on current home literacy activities. "He's older now and in preschool so I guess he would have learned anyway." When asked if she considered literacy events differently as a result of her time in the program, she appeared somewhat evasive. "Maybe when I was in the program, I did. But I'm not sure about now." When probed further, this mother did recognize that daily reading continued in her house, that she lets her son ask questions or make comments when they read together, that he helps her with grocery list making, that he reads alone from time to time, and that he writes his name on pieces of paper and sticks them everywhere. When it was suggested by the interviewer that perhaps these behaviors were a result of program participation, her acceptance of the idea was minimal. "Maybe, I'm not sure," she responded. In checking back to her initial interview, these behaviors did not seem to be among the home literacy repertoire. It is possible that the child's involvement with literacy had become so routine within the family that the parent's memory had become less clear. Similar views surfaced from other parents. Literacy events were usual in their homes, and the children were involved with print in a variety of ways. However, some parents were not willing to grant that the *Learning Together* program had influenced their home literacy activities.

Continued Influence of Program on Child Learning. Sixty-five percent of parents thought the *Learning Together* program had "set them on the right track," as noted by one mother. "It gave him confidence," commented another. "He used to be so shy and the program brought him out of himself. He is so much more social and I don't think that would have happened without going to the program." Another noted that her son "learned how to use words not his fists to get what he wanted. I remember the teacher telling the kids that in the program and I do it now."

Children loved it when their parents read to them. "We used to read a bit before the program and then all the time during the program. We do that now too," noted one mother. Many mentioned the names of their children's favorite books, an indication that some books were being read frequently to the children. "He knows that book by heart," responded a mother when she gave the title of her child's favorite book. He reads it to himself and to the baby. I just love it." Another parent commented that when they bring books home from the library, her daughter immediately "starts to make up the story from the pictures." Generally parents remarked on their children's interest in letters and words, on their desire to be read to, on their efforts to read and write themselves, on their demand for pencils, crayons and paper, on their knowledge of the alphabet, on their wishes to have their own literacy spaces such as a desk or table for their print objects, and their requests to have their writing and drawing efforts posted in the house. As one mother recounted, "My kid is really into this reading and writing. She is fascinated by the whole thing and wants to read and write. Sure we encourage her, but I think the program really had a good part to play in getting her interested in those things."

Other parents spoke of how important crafts were in their home. "They did a lot of that in the program," said one mother, "and she still asks me to do those kinds of things with her." Other parents held similar views about hands-on activities and games. "We've made crafts from all her favorite books," remarked one parent. Another mother maintained that craft making was an enduring part of her daughter's learning. "When we read a book together, she often asks 'What can we make from this story?' I'm beginning to run out of ideas and supplies," she laughed.

Some parents judged that the program no longer had an effect on their learning. "It was so long ago," commented one father. "I think she probably has forgotten what she did there." Another parent observed that the child's learning for literacy was more a result of what the parent was doing rather than what she had learned in the program. "They read books and sang songs and things," she noted. "But I think it is my efforts, not the program, that makes a difference now." One parent was quite adamant when she remarked that "the program was good" for her daughter but that the child was much younger then and that she has "to provide much more interesting things for her to do." Therefore, she bought readiness books at the local grocery store and her daughter now "traces letters and joins matching things in that book; and she can color in it too." In this mother's view, such activities were much more attuned to the child's needs than the literacy events provided in the child program.

Continued Influence of Program on Adult Learning. Over 65% of parents indicated that the program continued to influence their own learning. "I have so much more confidence to try things now," said one parent. "The program really boosted my morale and I have enrolled in a massage therapy course. I am much more independent." Other parents noted that "getting out to the *Learning Together* Program" was a first step in improving their circumstances. "It will be a bit of a juggle at times with the kids," said one mother. "But I want to improve myself and I know I can. So, I think I will take a teacher's aide course next year." Parents referred to other community programs they had enrolled in or were planning to participate in, such as *Brighter Futures.* This attention to their own future learning and/or the possibilities for potential employment surfaced frequently.

Parents also spoke about how what they learned in the program influenced their behaviors with other children in the family. "I know I will do a much better job with the new baby," commented one mother. "I am reading to her now and she is only six months. I would never have thought of doing that without the program." Another parent remarked upon how the knowledge she gained in the program has assisted her in helping the older child with homework. "I have some ideas to help him," she observed, "like brainstorming and really looking at words so you can remember how to spell them." Another mother recounted how, when her grade two child's report card indicated that she needed help with spelling, she was "able to ask the teacher intelligent questions" about what she could specifically do to help and the teacher gave her a handout on spelling which "was very useful. I don't think I would have been so brave to ask her before being in the program," she said.

Other parents commented on how they were much better at handling discipline in the home, having "picked up tricks about discipline in the program." "I don't lose my control as much," remarked one father. "I am much more aware of how kids learn and how I can step in before things get out of control." Another parent also spoke of her developing "sense of patience" and that she was much better "at finding things for the kids to do before supper time which is the worst time of the day in our house." Other parents spoke of playing games that requested the initial letter of objects with their child, singing songs in the car to deflect inappropriate behavior, asking for the child's input or assistance when using literacy such as posting a note on the fridge or writing grocery lists, or otherwise involving the child in literacy events around the house. "When the mail comes, I let her sort it, which one is for me, which one is for her dad. She's getting very good at it," remarked the mother. Another parent noted that sometimes when her children are getting really "antsy," she says "I need new pictures for the fridge. Draw me the best picture you have ever made. This gets them really involved before the roof blasts off the house."

Some parents did not think that their participation in the program continued to have an influence on their current learning. "Not really," said a mother, echoing the views of many of her peers. "It was good but once it was over, that was that for me." "For myself and my learning," noted another parent, "I don't think so. For what I do with my kids, yes, but not myself anyway." The perspective that continued learning for the adults did not persist confirms the concept that some of the participants did not expect to have a personal learning experience either during or after program participation.

While some parents noted that they were reading more themselves, many were of the opinion that their reading abilities had not changed. "I'm still a slow reader," commented one mother. "It just takes me ages to get through a book." Other participants reported that "reading is not my favorite thing," "I think I am about the same when it comes to comprehension," or "I still struggle with big words." However, as one parent noted, "I am reading more to my kids and it's a lot more fun thing to do, so I suppose I am getting better at it, but that's only with kids' books." Such perspectives demonstrate that the strategies they were using with their children when reading had not transferred to their own reading.

Exciting Reading Event in the Last Year. Over 80% of parents were able to identify a reading event demonstrated by their child that surprised or excited them during the year after program participation. The parents recounted these events with enthusiasm. They were impressed by their children's developing expertise and interest in reading, with several noting that such behaviors might not have been manifested if they had not participated in the program. Furthermore, the parents' skills at recognizing such behaviors as indications of the children's early attempts at reading reflect the adults' understanding of how children acquire literacy.

"She found two words in the store with her name – the beginning letter of her name – without me asking her," said one parent. "I was blown away." Another parent commented that her child loves Alpahagetti and picks out the letters she knows on her spoon. One mother recounted how her son has a book with an accompanying tape recording that he listens to in the car while he follows along in the book. "He asked to have recordings for his other books so that he can follow along with those too," she remarked. Several parents noted that their children requested books in the car so that they "could read and not get bored" during longer journeys. A parent told how she freezes vegetables in used sour cream containers that she labels to denote what vegetables they include. She asked her daughter to get some corn for supper. The child brought a container to her, stopped suddenly and said "This can't be corn. It doesn't have a C on it. I'll get the right one." Many parents spoke of their children having memorized stories, of being able to pick out the appropriate word from the pictures in the book when the adult reader paused, of recognizing words in the community, of knowing all the letters in the alphabet, and of choosing to include books in their play.

Exciting Writing Event in the Last Year. Approximately 86% of parents reported their children demonstrating writing ability, albeit at different levels of expertise depending on the age of the child. Interestingly, it appeared that the parents had provided writing materials that the children could access on their own and that their writing efforts were shared among family members. One mother reminisced how her son wanted "to make a card for someone," and that she was not to watch him. He went to his bedroom and after 20 minutes or so came back with the card. "This is for you, Mom," he said. It was a Mother's Day card, the drawing depicting flowers in a garden. Inside, the child had written "I lv u Mom." "I cried when I saw that," she recounted. "It was so special. I will keep that card forever." Another mother told of her child who after seeing a program on television about big cats made a book complete with drawings of a lion, tiger, and snow leopard. "Spell the words, for me, Mom," he requested and then he copied each word on the correct page of his book.

Parents spoke of their children writing letters or words in the snow or on the steamed windowpanes in the car. Several referred to their children writing their full names correctly for the first time. Others noted their children did drawings and told stories to accompany them. One child found a blank envelope and wrote the names of everyone in the family on it and said, "This letter is for everyone." Several children painted pictures and wrote their names "at the bottom like real painters do," as noted by one child. Several children made booklets, others made lists of things they wanted for birthday or Christmas presents. Other children wrote labels on items to denote ownership. One example shows a child who was tired of his brother taking his crayons and who wrote his own name in big letters on the box. One parent commented, "She has her own style of making letters. She makes the K (a letter in the child's name) by doing the right side lines first. It's amazing watching her figure it out."

The parents remarked that the children were "very keen on writing" or "love to write all the time." A mother noted that sometimes when she asks her child what she would like to do, she invariably says "writing" and that this child had used up "tons of paper" with letters and words she knows or copies from magazines. Most parents also maintained that they post their children's writings on the fridge or other location in the house.

Second Follow-Up Interview

With the addition of questions dealing with school life, the same interview questions were used for the second follow-up interview that took place approximately one year after the first follow-up interview. Here again, family circumstances had changed. Changes included new babies welcomed into the home, movement to new locations, financial situations modified as a result of lost jobs or found part-time or full time positions, the death of an elder family member, grave illness on the part of children, and the children's enrollment in formal education. Percentages were similar for parents' impressions about the continued positive influence of the program they received two years ago (56%), the influence of that program on the literacy activities in the home (65%), and the continued demonstration of the children's reading and writing development (80% and 86% respectively). One may conclude from these results that home-based literacy experiences were well established and continued to provide a solid foundation for the children to branch out into more extended and complicated literacy episodes.

Several parents mentioned that they were taking upgrading classes and moving out into the community. Thirty percent were enrolled in some type of course such as teacher aide, practical nursing, senior aide assistant, or other career-building education endeavor. Others had taken part-time work such as waitressing or clerking with local businesses. Many of the parents were moving out into the community now that their children were older and attempting to build career opportunities for themselves.

Adults' Reflections on Their Own Reading and Writing. Over 60% noted that reading for pleasure was a usual event for them. "I'm into novels, now," said one mother. "I've read at least three this past year." Another mother referred to the pleasure of the solitude of reading when she noted, "I just love it when I get a chance to just sit down and read *my* book (her emphasis). I don't hear a thing; I just get lost in the story." Several of her peers commented that now that their children were older, they had greater opportunity to read for themselves. "The kids are getting better at helping out so our house is less chaos now," commented one parent. "I often get a chance to read a magazine or book for myself during the day. That didn't happen when they were small." Several adults spoke of reading the newspaper every day, of borrowing books from the library, of buying magazines, and of sharing book information with others. "I gave my girl friend one of the books I read, "remarked one mother. "I couldn't wait for her to read it so we could talk about it." Such views differ quite strongly from those offered on the same topic during the first follow-up interview when many considered reading a tedious and tiresome task. Generally, most participants seemed to have a positive attitude toward reading, were taking advantage of opportunities to read for their own enjoyment, and were becoming more eclectic in their choice of texts.

Several adults mentioned they wrote in journals, often as a therapeutic way to cope with daily stress. "My counselor told me to write down how I felt, and that's the writing I do most often," commented a parent. "My spelling is awful but no one sees it but me," she laughed. Another parent described how journal writing was part of the *Learning Together* program. "We used to write down our thoughts after the joint sessions," she said. "I liked doing that so now I write down my thoughts about once a week, about the family and what is happening to us. It's like a diary, I suppose and it's fun to go back and read what I wrote once in a while. I think I will put photographs in it next." Comments such as these reflect the personal satisfaction participants derive from their writing and the act of writing helps them clarify their thinking. Interestingly however, only

35% of participants considered writing in this vein. Most reported that they did not write except for the infrequent note, list, letter, or card.

Parents who had younger children who had not been in the program indicated that they felt well prepared to involve their children in literacy events. "I read to my baby," said one mother. I never did that before with any of them when they were that small." Other parents commented that their children who had participated in the program often read with younger siblings and that the older children "must have picked something up from me as they do it the same way I do like pointing to the pictures, asking questions, and things." In other words, the influence of program participation appears to endure in those families where new or younger members could benefit.

Parents' Reflections on Children's Learning. Several parents noted that they continued to go back to their program binder for ideas to involve their children in literacy events. Some recounted how they modified and extended these ideas now that their children were older. Making crafts and other hands-on activities were maintained; bedtime story reading was a habitual event; library visits usually occurred a couple of times a month for 75% of participants. Furthermore, the children's repertoire of books expanded as a result of community library visits, the purchasing of books and the children's access to school library collections. As one parent noted, "When I think back on the program, it got me to do the things that would help my child. Like, a better way of reading with her, and showing her all the print that is around us. I would never have got on that track if I hadn't been in the program and now I see how well she is doing at school." Other parents presented similar views. "My kid is so much more advanced than others in his class," commented one father. "He's got so much information from books that we read." Another remarked that her child is "a sponge just soaking up what she is learning in school."

The data also suggest that parents were very aware of their children's continued interest in and interactions with literacy. Similar to the first follow-up interview, over 80% were able to identify a special reading event that their children demonstrated in the past year. Such events included the children reading a book alone, reading a book to a family member, asking for the correct spelling of words, requesting that particular words be pointed out to them in a book, and being able to "suss out words" on their own, as noted by one mother. Comparable percentages to the first follow-up interviews were also recorded for the writing efforts of their children (86%). There did not seem to be any doubt in the parents' minds that the children were continuing to progress appropriately in their literacy development. Perhaps even more important, parents clearly indicated their joy and pride in this development. In short, the children's literacy efforts often appeared to be an important part of family life with the result that home literacy events moved the children to more sophisticated literacy learning.

However, 30% of parents did not feel that participation in the *Learning Together* program continued to influence their children's literacy development. "It was good when he was there," commented one mother. "But that was so long ago, I think what he learned there is well gone. He's at school now and that's what's teaching him." Another parent remarked her child had now spent a whole year in kindergarten and that he had "gone well beyond what he learned in the program." The program appeared to suit these parents needs at the time of participation, but the effects did not linger. It is possible that the parents were considering only the child component of the program and were inattentive to their own efforts to involve their children in literacy events that may not have happened if they had not attended the program.

School Connections. By this second interview period, the majority of the children were already enrolled in kindergarten, or grade one. Over 80% of parents considered their children to be doing well in their first steps into formal education. They noted that their children liked school, had made friends there, "loved the teacher," and generally seemed to be progressing appropriately. The parents spoke of their children's homework tasks, many of which included letter or word tracing on photocopied sheets, spelling, word or number matching, coloring, writing sentences, or the home reading program depending on the age of the child. The latter assignment consisted of the children bringing home a simple book to read each day to their parents. "His home reading program makes sure that he reads every day," remarked one parent. "We listen to him read it and then sign a sheet that says he did it." Another parent noted that "he gets lots of reading now with his home reading books." Most parents took the homework assignments seriously, and although some noted that getting the children to do their homework was often "a chore at the end of the day" when the children were "tired and exhausted," they realized the necessity of completing the tasks so that the children could progress in school.

Over 80% of the parents had met their child's teacher, several had visited the school on numerous occasions, generally during parent-teacher interviews. These interactions reinforced their views that their children were progressing appropriately; any problems mentioned by the teachers appeared to be minor in their opinions such as "paying attention more," "waiting for his turn," or "remembering to bring back his reading book." One parent noted that now that she has more free time, she volunteers in the school about once a week. "This has been a real eye-opener for me;

the teachers, all of them, are just fantastic with the kids. I don't know how they keep their patience." Another parent picked up on this point when she recounted how concerned her child's teacher was when he was injured during recess. "She phoned me every day for three days to see that he was okay," she commented. Other parents remarked on the quantity of work their children had done in school. "He doesn't bring home much," said one mother, "But his scribblers in school are just full of things he has done. I couldn't get over how much work he had done, pages and pages." Overall, parents thought their children were learning in school, were accepted socially, and that school "was a good place" for them. They also were of the opinion that the school recognized their worth as parents and that they were major contributors to their children's learning. As one parent noted, "The teacher really listened to my questions. She told me how I could help Joanna get better as a reader – like reading the book over alone and looking at the pictures before she reads it to me with her home reading book." Several parents echoed this view of teacher-parent collaboration.

A few parents mentioned that their children who had been in the *Learning Together* program did not appear to have similar problems with school tasks that older siblings had experienced. "He's sailing through," commented one mother. He's got no problems, no ADHD like his older brother. I wish he had had the program too and maybe he wouldn't be having so much problem with math and reading." Another reported that, although her daughter struggles with math, her reading progress was good; she attributed that progress to what she, the mother, had learned about helping kids with reading in the *Learning Together* program.

It would appear from these comments that the majority of parents viewed their children's school experiences favorably and considered school a good place for their children to be. For those parents whose own school experiences had not been so constructive, their desire for their children to do well in school was being realized. Perhaps even more important, their own perspectives of schooling were changing as a result of their children's early success in school.

Community Programs. Nearly 75% of parents indicated they would like some course, similar to the *Learning Together* program for older children. "It would be great to have something after school for the kids and us parents as the kids get older and have to do harder stuff in school," remarked one mother. Other parents confirmed this view when they talked about helping their children with comprehension questions, math problems, writing, and spelling. The desire to continue to be involved with their children's learning and to assist them when necessary surfaced frequently within this interview period. "We need like a Step Two Learning Together," commented one father. "Like learning how to help with homework so it doesn't become a fight with the kids. I think the teachers could tell us more about helping our kids. They just say 'Help' but I don't know what they mean."

Now that their children were older, over 60% of the children were enrolled in some kind of community program such as Scouts, Beavers, swimming, skating, or crafts. This involvement in community events served as a social learning environment for the children. As one parent claimed, "He's able to learn how to get along with others better now that he's in Beavers. It's not like school where he has to sit all day. In Beavers, they do all sorts of things and he can play with the other kids. He just loves it." Other parents felt that these community programs allowed their children to learn things that would not occur in school. "She's earning her badges," commented one mother. "She knows she has to work hard to get them. They don't have things like that in school."

The reason why some children were not enrolled in community programs appeared to be the cost of these programs. Several parents mentioned the fact that they could not afford such opportunities. "They cost a lot," said one mother. "With three kids, we just can't afford it." However, many of these parents took advantage of community events that did not entail a financial burden, such as parades, library story time or reading programs, community picnics, playing in the local park, or walks at Christmas time to see the lights in the neighborhood. "We find lots to do," remarked a parent. "Just taking the dog for a walk is a lot of fun." Some parents also took advantage of the range of community programs available to them. They enrolled in photography, pottery, crafts, sewing, decorating, skating, cooking, woodwork, and other such classes. One woman was taking a children's book writing class. "I've read so many books to the kids," she said, "I thought I'd try my hand at it. But it's so hard."

Summary

By the time of the second interview, the participating families had grown in their knowledge about literacy. The majority of the *Learning Together* program children were enrolled in school and generally doing well in the opinion of the parents. As their children grew older, the demands on parental time were less constrained with the result that the adults had more time for personal reading and community involvement from the point of view of both career development and personal enhancement. Although several parents considered the influence of the *Learning*

Together program had dissipated, they still thought that the program helped them see how their children's literacy progresses and how to continue to help them. The majority of parents thought there was a need for an extension program, similar to the *Learning Together* program but one that would address the needs of older children.

Third Follow-Up Interview

The questionnaire for this interview was similar to that of the second interview. Information dealing with the influence of the *Learning Together* program on the children's development and the adults' own reading and writing, together with questions concerning the children's progress in school and the role of the community in family life, were recorded. There was little difference in parents' responses to the third and second follow-up interviews for most of the questions posed. However, school life took a much more prominent role in the responses to the third follow-up interview. At this period of data collection, family life was generally surrounded by school life.

Nevertheless, some interesting differences did surface across the two interviews. For example, while library visits occurred usually twice a month during the second interview-reporting period for 75% of participants, this percentage dropped to approximately 35% during the last interview. Many parents thought that the children's home reading program and their opportunity to select books from the school library collections were sufficient for the children's needs. "We don't go to the library much now," commented one mother. "She gets books at the school that she likes and reads them." Another referred to the home reading program as "taking a lot of time in the evening" to complete, with the result that the shared reading her daughter had experienced when younger now did not occur any more. Yet another mother noted that her grade two child "had piles of homework that takes hours to do each night" with the result that there was little time anymore for "just reading." Such comments reflect how school sometimes, for some children, creates perceived barriers in the way of literacy development. While it is agreed that school libraries have good collections for children, the borrowing rate is generally low, with only one book allowed per week. Such a system does not allow for the breadth of reading experiences that children access through public libraries. In addition, the quantity of homework may mitigate the development of the life long reading habits that evolve when children read their own choice of text for pleasure and enjoyment on a daily basis. However, the parents took school activities very seriously and tried their best to meet the academic standards set for their children.

Another difference that surfaced in this third interview concerned the children's progress. While over 80% believed that their children were doing well in school during the second interview period, this number dropped to 60% at the third interview. Some parents seemed both surprised and disappointed when they were informed that their children's progress was less than satisfactory. "I just couldn't believe it," mentioned one parent. "She seemed to be doing so well, and now they tell me she is having problems with comprehension and things. How could that happen?" Another parent reflected that "all the time we spent reading together is not paying off now. I just don't understand it." To compound problems, these parents were unsure of what to do, or what assistance they could give their children. In addition, a few commented on the fact that the teachers could not provide them with specific information for helping their children. "He's got to focus more," said one parent. "How do we teach him that?" Another complained that the school was "taking ages to have her son tested for learning disabilities. They don't even know if they can get him in this year," she remarked. Coupled with these observations concerning the children's progress, some parents indicated their frustrations either with the school or teacher, or with their own lack of knowledge concerning how best to alleviate their children's learning problems. "She wasn't helpful at all," noted one parent about her child's teacher. "She just said he would have to apply himself to get better grades." Another commented that the reason her child was having difficulty at school was as a result of there being so many children in the class. "There was talk of splitting the class into two," she said. "But that didn't happen and so now she (her daughter) just doesn't get enough attention. It's the old story." Yet another parent commented that she wished she could help her son more with his schoolwork. "But I don't know how to help (her emphasis). If I could afford it I would get a tutor or send him to one of those classes you see advertised on TV like Sylvan." One father mentioned that his daughter used to love to go to school but that now she says she hates it. "She has problems answering questions written down; that's what she hates the most about school."

On the other hand, for those parents whose children were succeeding, they were enthusiastic in their praise for the school. "The principal often talks to me when I go to pick up my kids," commented one mother. "She knows the names of all the kids; it's a wonder!" Other parents spoke of their children becoming independent readers and writers and of the difficulty and complexity of the texts they were reading and writing. "She wrote a four page story," noted one parent. "It was amazing and only had three spelling mistakes. I was so proud. We put the whole thing on our fridge." Another mother described how her daughter brought home a chapter book and that she "could read most of it herself." Their pride and pleasure in their children's achievements were evident in their comments.

Whether their children's success was an outcome of their time in the *Learning Together* program was more difficult for parents to determine. "It's hard to know," said one parent. "Maybe because we spent so much time reading and talking together over the years has paid off. We learned in the program that it was important to share things with kids so maybe we do more of that still in our house. I'm not sure though." Another mother commented that she and her husband had made reading a first priority in their family as a result of program participation and that this focus continued over the years. "Maybe without the program I wouldn't have," she observed. "We didn't before the program but they were so little then. I really don't know. It's hard to say."

Comments about their own learning were less ambiguous. "Definitely," mentioned one parent. "I learned a lot about discipline and how to deal with my kids in a better way in the program. That was the best for me." "I learned to have more patience," reported another parent, "and to listen to my kids better. And I watch for those things that show me how and what they are learning." Several parents remarked that the children often surprised them with their new knowledge about print. Examples included the children's awareness of the use of capital letters, writing notes to family members and friends, reading independently an unknown book for the first time, the inclusion of simple chapter books in their repertoire, reading independently what others have written such as notes on the fridge, and sharing the events in a story they had read. "I watch out for the new things to show up," said one parent. "I feel like I am on the journey with them as they learn."

Summary

Although the data collected from this third interview period replicated to a great degree the information collected earlier, some variations were evident. Fewer of the children appeared to be successful in school, a matter that was causing the parents of these children some concern. In addition, homework tasks interfered to a degree with the practice of shared reading in the home. Furthermore, families seemed to be less frequent users of the public library; the school library appeared to be the major source for the children's reading materials. Finally, parents were unsure of the continued influence of the *Learning Together* program on their children's learning. However, the practices put into place by the parents (e.g., discipline, awareness of the children's learning) as a result of their own program participation continued to be part of their family routines.

Introduction to Families in the Control Group

The participants who elected to serve as control subjects were interviewed at intervals similar to those individuals who participated in the *Learning Together* program. Like their program peers, these control subjects were interviewed in their homes, local community centres, restaurants or other mutually agreed locations. The control participants were given the opportunity to enroll in the program at a later stage if they wished, an opportunity for which only two control participants took advantage. Generally, reasons for non-participation included the continued illness of a family member in need of constant care, the demands of their work place situation, the perception that they did not have need of such a program, or the time constraints of the program did not meet their current life styles. However, as the study progressed, many continued to profess interest in the program and thought they might enroll during some future period if it were available.

Interviews with these parents did not result in the same breadth of information as with the intervention group, an understandable fact given that the program content and its influence on both parents and children provided greater opportunities for discussion. However, the control parents were very willing to share information about their own and their children's lives over the course of the *Learning Together* study and did their best to provide specific data about home literacy events. They received a $100 honorarium for each interview conducted.

First Interview

Like their program peers, the control group parents expressed similar views about their own school experiences. Forty percent maintained that this period of their life was enjoyable; they felt accepted in the school community, and if they had not had an unexpected pregnancy or other event such as the family moving, they likely would have graduated. The majority, however, were less fortunate. In the words of one mother who captured the sentiments of many of her peers, "School was miserable. I hated it." Generally such views included reasons as, "the wrong clothes," lack of friends, missing school because of illness or family responsibilities, "not doing well in class," and bullying and teasing. Some of the parents had returned to school later in life but, even then, academic tasks were a challenge.

Over 60% noted that they did not avail of the public library. "It's too far away," commented one mother, "and I don't have a car." Another noted that "going to the library is hairy with three small children. I feel the kids will do something wrong all the time, so it's just not worth it." However, 65% reported that they read to their children, usually a couple of times a week. In addition, these parents reported that their children had several books available to them, although only 30% could identify the name of their children's favorite book. Furthermore, 68% indicated that generally few writing events occurred in the home.

That the parents were involved with their children was obvious by the range of activities they shared with them – telling stories, going on outings, singing songs, playing games, drawing and painting, etc. While sometimes overburdened with the daily demands of caring for young children, parents enjoyed being with their children and frequently pondered how best to prepare them for future formal schooling. Over 40% of parents noted that for those slightly older children (four years of age and older), they availed of what could best be termed as "readiness" books found in local grocery stores in order to sensitize their children to literacy. Tracing letters, matching objects, coloring, and drawing were the usual activities completed from these texts. "I'm making sure he knows his ABCs," commented one mother. Few parents indicated that reading to their children served as a launch pad to literacy learning.

Second Interview

The second interview took place about four months after the initial interview. This interview focused primarily on parent-child joint activities, and the children's reading and writing behaviors. Parents involved their children in a variety of activities – playing with them, watching TV together, going for walks, doing crafts, shopping, making up stories for them, doing puzzles, and letting them assist with household chores. One parent echoed the views of many of her peers when she noted that her child "was a great help around the house. We spend a lot of time talking and working together."

Over 60% of parents were able to identify specific examples of their children's attempts in literacy such as writing their names, copying words, pretend reading to dolls or pets, asking for paper and pencil to write lists, and drawing. Most parents indicated that they were not involved with their child during these activities. "She just gets the stuff and does it on her own," commented one mother. "I let her be." However, some interviewer notes pointed out that several families had posted the children's drawing and writing on the kitchen refrigerator.

Older children in school appeared to influence the literacy events of their younger siblings. Over 30% of parents mentioned that the children played school together with the older child "acting the teacher" by showing the younger one "how to print letters and numbers and color in the lines," reading together with the older child asking questions or "cutting and pasting." Parents seemed to enjoy watching these events and commented upon how much the younger child was learning.

Forty percent of parents reported reading daily to their children. One mother reported to the interviewer, "Since you were here last and talking about reading and writing, I thought I'd better get more books, so I went to the Dollar store so we have lots now to read every day and not always the same ones." Over 50% maintained, as in the first interview, that they continued to read to their children a couple of times a week. Frequent library visits, however, continued to be rare.

In reference to their own literacy events, 70% of parents spoke of the functional aspects of reading and writing. Comments usually referred to making shopping lists, paying bills, writing notes on the calendar, checking the TV guide, reading recipes, sending cards to friends and relatives, and writing cheques. Few mentioned reading novels or magazines for their own enjoyment. However, 20% cited daily Bible reading as their main personal reading event. A similar number mentioned keeping a journal.

Third Interview (First Year Follow-Up)

This interview occurred one year after the second interview. Again, questions focused primarily on the children's reading and writing behaviors and on how the parents were encouraging their literacy development. For those parents for whom the target child was in formal education (usually kindergarten), the responses were much more detailed than in previous interviews and more comprehensive than those of the parents whose children had not started school.

Over 60% of parents noted that their children talked a great deal about school, the friends they played with, the teacher, who got in trouble, the things they did in school, and their snack, or other children's lunches.

One parent commented that her child "talks non-stop for an hour when she gets home. I tell her she is my little newspaper, she gives me all the news." Parents indicated they continued to be involved in a variety of activities with their children such as outings, camping, playing games, working on the computer, and drawing and writing, all of which generated considerable discussion. In addition, 35% of parents noted their children were enrolled in some community sports program such as swimming or skating.

Parents talked of the children's home reading program, which for 45% had somehow replaced their own reading to the child. The children had access to the school library, which meant that new books arrived weekly into the home. Sixty percent of parents were able to identify their child's favorite book, a 30% increase from the first interview. Furthermore, 50% commented that their children asked about words in a book. According to the parents, 80% of the children were able to write their own names; 30% noted the children could write several words. Some of the children who were enrolled in grade one had published their own little books, "complete with author and title page," as noted by one father. Forty percent of parents commented that their children liked to write and often left little notes around the house. "You can't really read them," said one parent, "but you know it says something."

When asked how they were assisting their children in their literacy development, parents generally appeared to take a passive role. "I'll help if they ask," said one parent, "but mostly I just let him get on with it." Such a view was expressed by 65% of parents. Other parents gave comments such as, "I listen to her home reading book when she reads it and tell her a word if she gets stuck," or "I ask him to sound out the word." Only 20% of parents mentioned providing the child with several strategies such as looking at the pictures for clues to the word or predicting what the word might be from its context and then verifying its accuracy. One mother put it succinctly when she noted: "I don't know what is the best thing to do and I don't want to confuse her so I just spell the word that she's struggling with. It seems to work." Other parents mentioned that they make sure books and other print materials such as paper and pencils are available to their children. Other than that, many parents did not appear to be directly involved in helping their children develop more strategic behaviours.

Public library visits did not increase over the year for these families. Thirty percent of parents highlighted the fact that their children received books as presents, thereby increasing the home library collection. In addition, 40% of parents mentioned that books could be purchased through the school's Scholastic book program. However, the modeling of reading by adults in the home could best be termed as sparse as 65% of parents commented primarily on the functional aspects of their reading. The number of parents reading novels or magazines for pleasure scarcely increased. On the other hand, greater mention was made of daily newspaper reading (30%).

Thirty percent of parents indicated they thought their children were having some trouble with their reading development, a fact confirmed for a few by teacher interviews. They were concerned about their lack of growth. A few had bought *Leap Pad*, an electronic reading game that they thought might help, although, as one mother reported, "It is too soon to tell." Others noted they would "help their children with their phonics so they could become better readers." No parents mentioned that their children were having difficulty writing.

Fourth Interview (Second Follow-Up)

Interview questions were similar to those of the previous interview. Like those parents in the intervention group, family dynamics had changed. New babies were welcomed; elders had died; spouses lost jobs or took jobs in distant locations. In some families, both parents were now working, with the result that family routines had shifted to accommodate less parental time with the children. As well, all of the target children were now in formal education.

However, as with the previous interview, parents continued to talk with their children about friends, school and other events, play with them, share time in front of the TV, watch them at sports, discuss movies and books, and tell stories. In short, families managed to work through daily routines, mostly in a harmonious fashion. Visits were made more frequently to the schools and some parents volunteered there. Over 80% reported being aware of what their children's interests were, how they were doing at school, and what the children's favorite books were. Half of the parents were of the opinion that the school's home reading program was very time consuming. In particular, one mother commented, "It takes ages each night and now I have two of them doing it; especially with Brenda (the target child) who only wants to talk about the pictures." On the other hand, 60% of parents noted their children now ask questions about the books they read or texts read to them. "I think he picked that up at school," said one mother. "Before that, he would just sit and listen. Now he talks about what is going on in the book. Takes more time, but he likes it. He's older too so he understands more," she concluded.

Nearly 70% of parents were able to identify some particular reading event that occurred during the past year. Such events included decoding words in the environment, showing words known in a book, reading a book from memory, remembering what a word is from seeing it just once, or reading to a younger sibling, to mention only a few of those reported. Parents were impressed by their children's abilities and used words and phrases such as "smart," "good student," "wants to learn," "interested in knowing the right words" and ""keen to understand" to explain their children's behaviors. Parents were even more specific about writing, with several of them having kept samples of their children's writing efforts. One parent reported how her kindergarten child spent hours marking his name on all his possessions with a black marker. Others reported, for example, that their children wrote notes and lists, made their own Christmas cards, or copied a whole class list for invitations to a birthday party. One parent noted that her daughter wrote her a note saying 'I'm sorry' after she got in trouble for teasing her younger sister. When asked by her mother how she knew how to spell 'sorry', she replied that she had copied it from a game in the closet.

Sixty-five percent of parents said their children were improving as readers and writers. However, even within that group, several confided that their children's progress was slower than they thought it might have been. "I shouldn't have to help her so much now that's she in Grade 2," commented a parent. "She should be able to do most of it by herself." Another parent referred to her son's interest in being a reader but that "he has the attention of a flea so he gets distracted so easily." She felt that keeping the child on task was harder than the task itself. A minority (30%) of parents were concerned about their children's level of achievement, however. "He tries to remember all the words," said one mother. "His phonics aren't good." Another considered that her child had only memorized words which she did not consider really reading. "She can only read what she's read many times before," she said. "Anything new and she has real trouble." The parents of these children had discussed the children's reading with their teacher but were still unsure of how to assist the children. The children's writing was of lesser concern, although 45% mentioned that spelling was a problem. Comments such as, "He's a messy writer," or " His printing is not the best" gives credence to the perception that penmanship is a more important focus for writing than the creation of ideas.

As with previous interviews, visits to public libraries were limited, and in 50% of cases were rare. Parents continued to rely on the availability of texts from school sources including the library or Scholastic purchase plan. Furthermore, their own reading and writing habits as adults mirrored those behaviors reported earlier in which reading and writing tasks were accomplished to get through the routines of the day. Only 30% spoke of reading books for their own enjoyment, again with the exception of biblical texts. In addition, newspaper reading had become slightly more prevalent in these homes at 40% and occurred several times a week.

Control Group Summary

In summary, the control group parents reported being involved with their children over the course of the study. They included their children in family activities, interacted with them in positive ways and generally thought that their children were developing appropriately. They noted that their children engaged in literacy activities in the home but, on the other hand, their own participation in these activities could best be described as passive. Several of the control group parents read frequently to their children during the course of the study. However, when the children were enrolled in school, their shared reading by and large was replaced by the school home reading program which many parents reported as tedious. Most of the adults' own literacy efforts centred upon the more functional aspects of print thereby reducing their children's opportunity to observe their parents reading or writing for personal satisfaction. As the children were faced with the more formal literacy instruction of the school, many parents were concerned about their children's reading development which they thought was not as satisfactory as it should be. Although a few parents expressed interest in enrolling in the *Learning Together* program, it seems family circumstances generally prevented them from doing so.

Similarities between treatment and control groups

- Both groups expressed positive and realistic expectations for their children's future academic success.
- Both groups maintained that success in literacy achievement was a key to academic success.
- Both groups professed a desire for a better life for their children than their own.
- Both groups perceived that their lack of high school education was generally the result of poor choices on their part rather than extenuating circumstances.

- In spite of financial and educational difficulties, both groups considered they have the strength and fortitude, with the assistance of the community, to provide the best for their children.
- Both groups wished to extend their own educational standards when their children place fewer daily demands upon them.
- Both groups maintained that the "text world" of the school is a difficult one for learners.
- Both groups experienced difficult family circumstances.

Differences between treatment and control groups

- Treatment group parents manifested a broader language repertoire to describe their children's educational development in general, and literacy development in particular, than their control group peers.
- Treatment group parents demonstrated greater involvement in community programs over the course of the study than their control group peers.
- Control group parents maintained a traditional or mechanistic view of how literacy is acquired. Treatment parents spoke more frequently of a variety of strategies that enhance literacy development and paid particular attention to the personal enjoyment to be obtained from literacy events.
- Control group parents appeared less aware of the breadth of programs available to them within the community to assist them in raising their children.
- Once their children attended school, treatment group parents appeared to be more comfortable approaching school authorities than their control group peers.
- Treatment parents indicated greater extended family support for their children's literacy than did the control group parents.

Chapter Six
Conclusions and Policy Implications

The main objective of this study was to determine whether beneficial effects accrue from the use of and participation in the *Learning Together* program. Specifically, effects were sought on (1) children's literacy development, (2) parents' literacy development, and (3) parents' ability to assist in the development of their children's literacy. Other objectives included (4) the identification of the time to intervene in children's literacy development for the greatest effect; (5) the documentation of parents' contingent responsivity to scaffold their children's language; (6) the reporting of what parents say about their own literacy experiences and perceptions prior to, during, and after their participation in the program; and (7) the reporting of parents' observations about the literacy of their children now in school. The results of this study lead to several conclusions and policy implications.

Children's Literacy Development

The study confirmed the incredibly powerful combined effect of parents' education and parents' reading ability on their children's reading ability before starting school. This result points to the crucial importance of children finishing high school with commensurate literacy achievement. Educational policy makers should redouble efforts to promote the importance of school completion with appropriately corresponding levels of literacy.

The *Learning Together* program affected literacy development positively and no matter what the children's initial literacy level only at the posttest stage. In subsequent follow-up years, the program continued to have a positive influence for all children except those who were in the top 20% to 30% at the pretest stage. This result supports the conclusion that the *Learning Together* program should continue for those children at or below the 70th to 80th percentile on the pretest measure. In order to maximize the use of resources, children should be screened before entry into the program and recommended for admission only if their literacy levels suggest they would benefit. A national screening program of all preschool children would help ensure that the program reaches its intended target population.

Parents' Literacy Development

Ethnicity and native language proved to be significant predictors of parents' literacy level, but these are factors beyond anyone's control. More important than these was educational level, which was shown to be able to cancel out their negative effects. The results show that the children of parents with higher educational levels have higher literacy levels, and much of the benefit comes with high school completion. The results suggest that increasing the educational levels of parents with less than a high school education is the most effective means of increasing their literacy levels and a powerful means of increasing their children's. Policies and programs are needed that make it possible, feasible, and enticing for adults without high school education to enroll in upgrading. Given that adult literacy programs currently reach fewer than 10% of adults who need such programs, continued use of family literacy programs as a means to draw parents into further learning opportunities for themselves as well as their children is warranted.

Consistent with other studies documented in the literature review, no increase in parents' reading level attributable to the *Learning Together* program was found. In order to improve parents' literacy, a program is needed that makes that goal central. One possibility is to develop and assess a comprehensive and accredited adult learning program that builds upon current school-based programs.

Parents' Ability to Assist

The results showed that parents acquired and implemented more frequent and varied literacy activities in the home. Given the parents' enthusiasm and delight with what they learned from the *Learning Together* program, their requests for a more extensive program signals the need for programs to be longer in duration and directed toward varying levels of literacy attainment.

Best Time to Intervene

The results showed that the intervention worked the same for children no matter their beginning age from 36 to 60 months of age. What mattered was their beginning literacy level. Given the constant effectiveness of the *Learning Together* program across this age group, common sense dictates working with families as soon as possible.

Parents' Responsivity

The study confirmed that parents appreciated and felt empowered to learn strategies for engaging in and responding to their children's emergent literacy while in the *Learning Together* program. Seventy-five percent of parents in the post-program interviews requested a continuing or another program to help them to support the children's learning at school. Ongoing and sustained programs for parents are needed in order for parents to learn more sophisticated strategies to help their children as they progress through schooling.

Parents' Literacy Experiences

Parents in the *Learning Together* program reported being more confident and secure in their own abilities to help their children, reading more often, attending more to print, and engaging more with print in various forms. They expressed a desire to learn more ways to improve their own literacy level. The results point to the need for family literacy programs to more directly address the literacy needs of individual adults and to place more emphasis on increasing parents' literacy skills for their own benefit. Family literacy is about benefits for both adults and their children.

Parents' Observations of Their Children

The results support the conclusion that the parents in the *Learning Together* program acquired a language to talk about their children's literacy development, learned to make astute observations of their children's skills and abilities, adopted ways to extend and sustain their children's interests, and varied the breadth and depth of literacy within the family. The results again support ongoing family literacy programs to assist and instruct parents to maintain their significant role in the literacy development of their children.

Concluding Remarks

All of what we have reported may be summarized as support for an evidence-based program in family literacy. The longitudinal quasi-experimental and qualitative evaluation of the *Learning Together* program showed effectiveness for children with the greatest need, qualitative improvements in parents' ability to be able to advance the literacy levels of their children, and the express need for a greater focus on adult literacy advancement. Long-term research on families is necessary in order to study the barriers to sustained literacy development. We need to examine the impact on families of their participation in less intensive family literacy programs as well as the impact of programs such as *Learning Together* offered over a longer period of time. We need to examine ways to help teachers understand social and cultural differences and their effects on literacy development. We need to examine ways in which policy and practice can be integrated to best serve the whole child. Finally, we need research that helps us use our limited resources more efficiently by more accurately pinpointing which interventions work best for which groups and at what time.

References

Adams, M.J. (1990). *Beginning to Read*. Cambridge, MA: MIT Press.

ALBSU. (1993). *Parents and their children: The intergenerational effect of poor basic skills*. London: Adult Literacy and Basic Skills Unit.

Anderson, J., Anderson, A., Lynch, J., & Shapiro, J. (2003). Storybook reading in a multicultural society: Critical perspectives. In A. van Kleeck, S. Stahl, & E. Bauer (Eds.). *On reading books to children: Parents and teachers* (pp. 203-230). Mahwah, NJ: Lawrence Erlbaum Associates.

Anderson, R.C., Hiebert, E.H., Scott, J., & Wilkinson, I.A.G. (1985). *Becoming a nation of readers: The report of the Commission on Reading*. Washington, DC: National Institute of Education.

Auerbach, E.R. (1989). Towards a socio-contextual approach to family literacy. *Harvard Educational Review, 59,* 165-181.

Auerbach, E.R. (1995a). Deconstructing the discourse of strengths in family literacy. *Journal of Reading Behaviour, 27,* 643-661.

Auerbach, E.R. (1995b). Which way for family literacy: Intervention or empowerment. In L. Morrow (Ed.), *Family literacy connection in schools and communities* (pp. 11-28). Newark, DE: International Reading Association.

Barton, D., Hamilton, M. (1998). *Local literacies: Reading and writing in one community*. London: Routledge.

Bourgeois, P. (1993). *Canadian postal workers*. Richmond, Ontario: Scholastic.

British Columbia Women's Institute. (1892). *Modern pioneers*. Vancouver, BC: Evergreen Press Limited.

Brizius, J.A., & Foster, S.A. (1993). *Generation to generation: Realizing the promise of family literacy*. Ypsilanti, MI: High/Scope Press.

Brooks, G., Gorman, R., Harman, J., Hutchison, D., & Wilkin, A. (1996). *Family literacy works: The evaluation of the Basic Skills Agency's Demonstration Programmes.* London: The Basic Skills Agency.

Brown, Gay. (1984). *Games for vernacular preschools.* Ukarumpa via Lae, Papua New Guinea: Summer Institute of Linguistics.

Buchmann, M., & Schwille, J.R. (1993). Education, experience, and the paradox of finitude. In M. Buchmann & R.E. Floden (Eds.), *Detachment and concern* (pp. 19-33). New York: Teachers College Press.

Bus, A., & van Ijzendoorn, M., & Pellegrini, A. (1995). Joint book reading makes for success in learning to read: A meta-analysis on intergenerational transmission of literacy. *Review of Educational Research,* 65(1), 1-21.

Bynner, J. & Fogelman, K. (1993). Making the grade: Education and training experiences. In E. Ferri (Ed.), *Life at 33: The fifth follow-up of the National Child Development Study.* London: National Children's Bureau.

Campbell, P.M. & Brokop, F.M. (2000). *Canadian adult reading Assessment instructor's manual and CD-ROM.* Edmonton, AB: Grass Roots Press.

Canadian Education Statistics Council (2006). *Report of the Pan-Canadian education indicators program 2005.* Toronto, ON: Canadian Education Statistics Council.

Christie, J.F. (1991). Play and early literacy development: Summary and discussion. In J.F. Christie (Ed.). *Play and early literacy development* (pp. 233-246). Albany: State University of New York Press.

Conti-Ramsden, G. (1990). Maternal recasts and other contingent replies to language-impaired children. *Journal of Speech and Hearing Disorders,* 55, 262-274.

Delgato-Gaitan, C. (1996). *Protean literacy: Extending the discourse on empowerment.* London: Falmer Press.

Department of Education and Science, (DES). (1989). *English in the national curriculum.* London, HMSO.

DeTemple, J.M. (2001). Parents and children reading books together. In D.K. Dickinson & P.O. Tabors (Eds.), *Beginning literacy with language* (pp. 31-51). Baltimore, MD: Paul H. Brookes Publishing Company.

Dewey, J. (1966). *Democracy and education: An introduction to the philosophy of education.* New York: Free Press (Original work published 1916).

Dickinson, D.K. & Tabors, P.O. (Eds.). (2001). *Handbook of early literacy research.* New York: Guilford Publications.

Dickinson, D.K., & McCabe, A. (2001). Bringing it all together, the multiple origins, skills, and environmental supports of early literacy: Emerging skills and environmental supports. *Learning Disabilities Research and Practice, 16,* 186-202.

Doake, D. (1988). *Reading begins a birth.* Richmond Hill, Ontario: Scholastic.

Dunn, L.M. & Dunn, L.M. (1997). *Peabody picture vocabulary test (PPVT),* (3rd Ed., Form 111A). Circle Pines, MN: American Guidance Service.

Durkin, D. (1966). *Children who read early.* New York: Teachers College Press.

Dyson, AH (1989). *The multiple worlds of child writers: Friends learning to write.* New York: Teachers College Press.

Edmiaston, R.K., & Fitzgerald, L.M. (2003). Exploring even start and head start family literacy programs. In A. DeBruin-Parecki & B. Krol-Sinclair (Eds.), *Family literacy: From theory to practice* (pp. 168-183). Newark, DE: International Reading Association.

Edwards, P.A. (1989). Supporting lower SES mothers' attempts to provide scaffolding for book reading. In J. Allen and Mason J.M. (Eds.), *Risk makers, risk takers, risk breakers: Reducing the risks for young literacy learners.* Portsmouth, NH: Heinemann.

Edwards, P.A. (1991). Fostering early literacy through parent coaching. In E. Hiebert (Ed.), *Literacy for a diverse society* (pp. 199-213). New York: Teachers College Press.

Edwards, P.A. (1995). Combining parents, and teachers, thoughts about storybook reading at home and school. In L. Morrow (Ed.), *Family literacy connections in schools and communities* (pp. 54-69). Newark, DE: International Reading Association.

Epstein, J., & Connors, L. (2002). Family, school, and community partnerships. In M.H. Bornstein (Ed.), *Handbook of parenting,* (2nd ed.), (pp. 407-437). Mahwah, NJ: Lawrence Erlbaum Associates.

Evans, M.A., Shaw, D., & Bell, M. (2000). Home literacy activities and their influence on early literacy skills. *Canadian Journal of Experimental Psychology, 54(2),* 65-75.

Floden, R.E., & Buchmann, M. (1993). Breaking with everyday experience for guided adventures in learning. In M. Buchmann & R.E. Floden (Eds.), *Detachment and concern* (pp. 34-49). New York: Teachers College Press.

Foster M. A., Lambert, R., Abbott-Shim, M., McCarty, F., & Franze, S. (2005). A model of home learning environment and social risk factors in relation to children's emergent literacy and social outcomes. *Early Childhood Research Quarterly, 20,* 13-36.

Gadsden, V.L. (2000). Intergenerational literacy within families. In M.L. Kamil, P.B.Mosenthal, P.D. Pearson, & R. Barr (Eds.), *Handbook of reading research:* Volume III (pp. 871-887). Mahwah, NJ: Lawrence Erlbaum Associates.

Goodman, Y. (1984). The development of initial literacy. In H. Goelman, A.A. Oberg, & F. Smith (Eds.), *Awakening to literacy,* (pp. 102 -109). Portsmouth, NH: Heinemann.

Goodman, Y. (1986). Children coming to know literacy. In W.H. Teale & E. Sulzby (Eds.), *Emergent literacy: Writing and reading* (pp. 1-14). Norwood, NJ: Ablex Publishing Corporation.

Gregory, E. (2001). Sisters and brothers as language and literacy teachers: Synergy between siblings playing and working together. *Journal of Early Childhood Literacy, 1* (3), 301-322.

Griffiths, A. & Edmonds, M. (1986). *Report on the Calderdale pre-school parent book project.* Halifax, UK: School Psychological Service, Calderdale Education Department.

Hammer, C. S., Tomblin, J. B., Zhang, X. & Weiss, A. (2001). Relationship between parenting behaviors and specific language impairment in children. *International Journal of Language and Communication Disorders, 36,* 185-205.

Hannon, P. (1995). *Literacy, home and school: Research and practice in teaching literacy with parents.* Chichester, UK: Falmer.

Hannon, P., & James, S. (1990). Parents' and teachers' perspectives on pre-school literacy development. *British Educational Research Journal, 16,* (3), 259-72.

Hannon, P., Morgan, A., & Nutbrown, C. (2006). Parents' experiences of a family literacy programme. *Journal of Early Childhood Research, 4(1),* 19-44.

Harris, T.L. & Hodges, R.E. (Eds). (1995) *The literacy dictionary.* Newark, DE: International Reading Association.

Hayden, R., & Phillips, L.M. (2000). *The forecast is good: Report on the formative evaluation of the "Learning Together - Read and write with your child" program.* Ottawa: National Literacy Secretariat.

Heath, S.B. (1983). *Ways with words.* Cambridge, UK: Cambridge University Press.

Heath, S.B. (1991). The sense of being literate: Historical and cross-cultural features. In R. Barr, M.L. Kamil, P.B. Mosenthal, & P.D. Pearson, (Eds.), *Handbook of reading research:* Volume II (pp. 3-25). New York: Longman.

Hendrix, S. (1999). Family literacy education – Panacea or false promise? *Journal of Adult and Adolescent Literacy, 43(4),* 338-346.

Her Majesty's Inspectorate (HMI). (1989). *The education of children under five.* London: HMSO.

Hess, R.D. & Holloway, S. (1984). Family and school as educational institutions. In R.D. Parke (Ed.) *Review of Child Development Research* (pp. 179-222). Chicago: University of Chicago Press.

Hill, M. (1989). *Home: Where reading and writing begin.* Portsmouth, NH: Heinemann Educational Books.

Hinshaw, S. P. (1992). Externalizing behavior problems and academic underachievement in childhood and adolescence: Causal relationships and underlying mechanisms. *Psychological Bulletin, 111,* 127–155.

Huey, E.B. (1908). *The psychology and pedagogy of reading.* Cambridge, MA: The MIT Press.

International Reading Association (1999). High stakes assessments in reading: A position statement of the International Reading Association. *Reading Teacher, 53,* 257-264.

International Reading Association (2001). *What is family literacy?* Brochure. www.reading.org

Kagan S.L., Moore E., & Bredekamp S. (1995). *Reconsidering children's early development and learning: Toward common views and vocabulary.* Washington, DC: National Education Goals Panel.

Kamerman, S., & Kahn, J. (1997). *Family change and family policies in the West.* New York: Oxford University Press.

Keating, D., & Hertzman, C. (1999). *Developmental health and the wealth of nations: Social, biological, and educational dynamics.* New York: The Guilford Press.

Kendrick, M. (2003). *Converging worlds: Play, literacy and culture in early childhood.* New York: Peter Lang.

Kush, J. C., & Watkins, M. V. (1996). Long-term stability of children's attitudes toward reading. *Journal of Educational Research, 89,* 315-319.

Landry, S.H., & Smith, K.E. (2005). The influence of parenting on emerging literacy skills. In David K. Dickinson and Susan B. Neuman (Eds.). *Handbook of early literacy research.* (pp.135-148). New York: Guildford Press.

Lee, V.E. & Burkam, D.T. (2002). *Inequality at the starting gate.* Washington, DC: Economic Policy Institute.

Levin, I., Patel, S., Margalit, T., & Barad, N. (2002). Letter names: Effect on letter saying, spelling, and word recognition in Hebrew. *Applied Psycholinguistics, 2,* 269-300.

Locke, J.L. (1986). Pittsburgh's beginning with books project. *School Library Journal,* February, 22-24.

Long, E. & Middleton, S. (2001). *Patterns of participation in Canadian literacy programs.* Toronto, ON: ABC Canada

Long, E. & Middleton, S., (2001). *Who wants to learn? Patterns of participation in Canadian literacy and upgrading programs: Results of a national follow-up study.* Don Mills, ON: ABC Literacy Foundation.

Lonigan, C. J., Bloomfield, B. G., Anthony, J. L., Bacon, K. D., Phillips, B. M., & Samwel, C. S. (1999). Relations among emergent literacy skills, behavior problems, and social competence in preschool children from low- and middle-income backgrounds. *Topics in Early Childhood Special Education, 19(1),* 1-23.

Lonigan, C., Burgess, S.R., Anthony, J.L, & Barker, T.A. (1998). Development of phonological sensitivity in two-to-five-year-old children. *Journal of Educational Psychology, 90,* 294-311.

Lynch, R. (2004). *Exceptional returns: Economic, fiscal, and social benefits of investment in early childhood development.* Washington, DC: Economic Policy Institute (http://www.epinet.org)

McCormick, C., & Mason, J.M. (1986). Intervention procedures for increasing preschool children's interest in and knowledge about reading. In W. H. Teale & E. Sulzby (Eds.). *Emergent literacy,* (pp. 90-115). San Francisco, CA.

McKeough, A., Phillips, L., Timmons, V., & Lupart, J. (Eds.) (2006). *Understanding literacy development: A global view.* Mahwah, NJ: Lawrence Erlbaum Associates.

Mills, K. (1998). *Something better for my children: The history and people of Head Start.* New York: Dutton.

Morrison, F., Bachman, H, & Connor, C. (2005). *Improving literacy in America.* New Haven, CT: Yale University Press.

Morrow, L. (1989). *Literacy development in the early years.* Englewood Cliffs: Prentice-Hall.

Neuman, S.B. (1998). A social-constructivist view of family literacy. In E.G. Sturtevant, J. Dugan, P. Linder, & W.M. Linek (Eds.), *Literacy and community: The twentieth yearbook* (pp. 25-30). Carrollton, GA: The College Reading Association.

Neumann, S. (2005). The knowledge gap. In David Dickinson, & Susan B. Neumann (Eds.). *Handbook of early literacy research.* (pp.29-40). New York: The Guildford Press.

Neumann, S., & Roskos, K. (1993). Access to print for children of poverty: Differential effects of adult mediation and literacy enriched play settings on environmental and functional print tasks. *American Educational Research Journal, 30,* 95-122.

Newman, A.P., & Beverstock, C. (1990). *Adult literacy: Contexts and challenges.* Newark, DE: International Reading Association.

Nickse, R. (1989). *The noise of literacy: Overview of intergenerational and family literacy programs.* (Report No CE-053-282). Boston, MA: Boston University Press.

Nutbrown, C. & Hannon, P. (1997). *Preparing for early literacy education with parents: A professional development manual.* Nottingham: The REAL Project/NES Arnold Limited.

Nutbrown, C., Hannon, P., & Morgan, A. (2005). *Early literacy work with families.* London: Sage Publication Ltd.

Oakeshott, M. (1989). A place of learning. In T. Fuller (Ed.), *The voice of liberal learning: Michael Oakeshott on education* (pp. 17-42). New Haven, CT: Yale University Press. (Original work published 1975).

Paratore, J.R. (2001). *Opening doors, opening opportunities.* Needham Heights, MA: Allyn & Bacon.

Paratore, J.R. (2002). Family literacy. In B. Guzzetti (Ed.). *Literacy in America: An encyclopedia of history, theory, and practice* (pp. 185-187). Santa Barbara, CA: ABC-CLIO, Inc.

Pelletier, J., & Corter, C. (2005). Toronto First duty: Integrating kindergarten, childcare, and parenting support to help diverse families connect to schools. *Multicultural Education, 13*, 30-37.

Pelligrini, A.D., & Galda, L. (1991). Longitudinal relations among preschoolers' symbolic play, metalinguistic verbs, and emergent literacy. In J.F. Christie (Ed.). *Play and early literacy development* (pp. 47-67). Albany: State University of New York Press.

Phillips, L.M. & Sample, H.L. (2005). Family literacy: Listen to what the families have to say. In J. Anderson, M. Kendrick, T. Rogers, & S. Smythe (Eds.), *Portraits of literacy across families, communities and schools: Intersections and tensions* (pp. 91-107). Mahwah, NJ: Lawrence Erlbaum Associates.

Phillips, L.M., Norris, S.P., & Mason, J.M. (1996). Longitudinal effects of early literacy concepts on reading achievement: A kindergarten intervention and five-year follow-up. *Journal of Literacy Research, 28(1),* 173-195.

Prospects Literacy Association (2000). *Curriculum for learning together: Read and write with your child.* Edmonton, AB: Prospects Literacy Association (now, Centre for Family Literacy)

Purcell-Gates, V. (1993). Issues for family literacy research: Voices from the teachers. *Language Arts, 70,* 670-677.

Purcell-Gates, V. (2000). Family literacy. In M.L. Kamil, P.B. Mosenthal, P.D. Pearson, & R. Barr (Eds.), *Handbook of reading research*: Volume III (pp. 853-870). Mahwah, NJ: Lawrence Erlbaum Associates.

Purcell-Gates, V., & Dahl, K. (1991). Low SES children's success and failure at early literacy learning in skills based classrooms. *Journal of Reading Behavior, 23*, 1-34.

Ravid, D., & Tolchinsky, L., (2002). Developing linguistic literacy. *Journal of Child Language, 29*, 417-447.

Raz, I.S. & Bryant, P. (1990). Social background, phonological awareness and children's reading. *British Journal of Developmental Psychology, 8*, 209-225.

Reid, D.K., Hresko, W.P. & Hammill, D.D. (1989). *Test of early reading ability,* (2nd Ed.) Austin, TX: Pro-ed.

Reid, D.K., Hresko, W.P. & Hammill, D.D. (2001). *Test of early reading ability – 3*. Austin, TX: Pro-ed.

Rodriguez-Brown, F.V. (2003). Essay book review: Reflections on family literacy from a sociocultural perspective. *Reading Research Quarterly, 38(1),* 146-153.

Rodriguez-Brown, F.V., & Meehan, M.A. (1998). Family literacy and adult education: Project FLAME. In M.C. Smith (Ed.). *Literacy for the twenty-first century: Research, policy, practices, and the national adult literacy survey* (pp. 175-193). Westport, CT: Praeger Publishers.

Sample Gosse, H.L. & Phillips, L.M (2006). Family literacy in Canada: Foundation to a literate society. In A. McKeough, L. Phillips, V. Timmons, & J. Lupart (Eds.), *Understanding literacy development: A global view* (pp. 113-135). Mahwah, NJ: Lawrence Erlbaum Associates.

Saracho, O.N., & Spodek, B. (2005). *Contemporary perspectives on families, communities, and schools for young children.* Greenwich, CA: Information Age Publishing.

Scarborough, H., & Dobrich, W. (1994). On the efficacy of reading to preschoolers. *Developmental Review,14*, 245-502.

Scarborough, H.S., Dobrich, W., & Hager, M. (1991). Preschool literacy experience and later reading achievement. *Journal of Learning Disabilities, 24,* 508-511.

Scharer, N. (1993). *Emily's house.* Toronto, ON: Douglas & McIntyre.

Segel, E., & Friedberg, J.B. (1991). *Follow-up study of the impact of the Kenan Trust model for family literacy.* Louisville, KY: National Center for Family Literacy.

Sénéchal, M. (2006). Testing the home literacy model: Parent involvement in kindergarten is differentially related to grade 4 reading comprehension, fluency, spelling, and reading for pleasure. *Scientific Studies of Reading, 10(1),* 59-87.

Sénéchal, M., & LeFevre, J. (2002). Parental involvement in the development of children's reading skill: A five-year longitudinal study. *Child Development, 73(2),* 445-460.

Sénéchal, M., & LeFevre, J., Thomas, E., & Daley, K (1998). Differential effects of home literacy experiences on the development of oral and written language. *Reading Research Quarterly, 33(1),* 96-116.

Sénéchal, M., Thomas, E., & Monker, J. (1995). Individual differences in 4-year-old children's acquisition of vocabulary during storybook reading. *Journal of Educational Psychology, 87,* 218-229.

Serpell, R. (1997). Critical issues: Literacy connections between school and home: How should we evaluate them? *Journal of Literacy Research, 29,* 587-616.

Shaywitz, S.E., Fletcher, J.M., & Shaywitz, B.A. (1994). Issues in the definition and classification of attention deficit disorder. *Topics in Language Disorders, 14,* 1-25.

Smith, S.S., & Dixon, R. G. (1995). Literacy concepts of low- and middle-class four-year-olds entering preschool. *Journal of Educational Research, 88(4),* 243-253.

Snow, C. (1983). Literacy and language: Relationships during the preschool years. *Harvard Educational Review, 53(2),* 165-189.

St. Pierre, R.G., Gamse, B., Alamprese, J., Rimdzius, T., & Tao, F. (1998). *National evaluation of the Even Start family literacy program: Evidence from the past and a look to the future.* Washington, DC: U.S. Department of Education Planning and Evaluation Service.

Stainthorp, R., & Hughes, D. (2000). Family literacy activities in the homes of successful young readers. *Journal of Research in Reading, 23 (1),* 41-54.

Sticht, T. (personal communication, February 14, 2006). Stopping functional illiteracy at its sources: A life cycles education policy perspective.

Sticht, T., & McDonald, B. (1989). *Making the nation smarter: The intergenerational transfer of literacy.* San Diego, CA: Institute for Adult Literacy.

Sulzby, E. (1991). The development of the young child and the emergence of literacy. In J. Flood, J.M. Jensen, D. Lapp, and J.R. Squire (Eds.). *Handbook of research on teaching the English language arts* (pp.273-285). New York: Macmillan.

Sulzby, E., & Teale, W. (1991). Emergent literacy. In R. Barr, M.L. Kamil, P. Mosenthal, & P.D. Pearson (Eds.), *Handbook of reading research*: Vol. II (pp. 727-758). Mahwah, NJ: Lawrence Erlbaum Associates.

Swinson, J. (1985). A parental involvement project in a nursery school. *Educational Psychology in Practice, 1(1)*, 19-22.

Taylor, D. (1983). *Family literacy: Young children learning to read and write.* Portsmouth, NH: Heinemann.

Taylor, D., & Dorsey-Gaines, C. (1988). *Growing up literate: Learning from inner-city families.* Portsmouth, NH: Heinemann.

Taylor, D. & Strickland, D.S. (1986). *Family storybook reading.* Portsmouth, NH: Heinemann.

Taylor, D., & Strickland, D. (1989). Learning from families: Implications for educators and policymakers. In J.B. Allen & J.M. Mason (Eds.), *Risk makers, risk takers, risk breakers: Reducing the risks for young literacy learners* (pp. 251-280). Portsmouth, NH: Heinemann.

Teale, W.H. (1986). Home background and young children's literacy development. In W.H. Teale & E. Sulzby (Eds.), E*mergent literacy: Writing and reading* (pp. 173-206). Norwood, NJ: Ablex.

Teale, W.H., & Sulzby, E. (Eds.), (1986). *Emergent literacy: Writing and reading.* Norwood, NJ: Ablex.

Thomas, A., Fazio, L., & Stiefelmeyer, B. (1999a). *Families at school: A guide for educators.* Newark, DE: International Reading Association.

Thomas, A., Fazio, L., & Stiefelmeyer, B. (1999b). *Families at school: A guide for parents.* Newark, DE: International Reading Association.

Tinsley, B.J. (2003). *How children learn to be healthy.* Cambridge, UK: Cambridge University Press.

Torres, R. M. (2003). The fundamental linkages between child, youth and adult learning and education. http://www.iizdvv.de/englisch/-Publikationen/Supplements/60_2003/eng_someconclusionsandelements.htm

Tracey, D.H. (1995). Family literacy: Overview and synthesis of an ERIC search. In E. Hinchman, D. Leu, & C. Linzer (Eds.), *Perspectives on literacy: Research and practice* (pp. 280-288). Forty-fourth Yearbook of the National Reading Conference. Chicago: National Reading Conference.

Wade, B. (1984). *Story at home and school. Educational review publication, # 10.* Birmingham, UK: University of Birmingham, Faculty of Education.

Wagner, R.K., & Torgensen, J.K. (1987). The nature of phonological processing and its causal role in the acquisition of reading skills. *Psychological Bulletin, 101,* 192-212.

Wasik, B.H., Dobbins, D.R., & Herrmann, S. (2001). Intergenerational family literacy: Concepts, research, and practice. In S.B. Neuman, & D.K. Dickinson, (Eds.), *Handbook of early literacy research* (pp. 444-458). New York: The Guilford Press.

Weinberger, J. (1996). *Literacy goes to school.* London: Paul Chapman.

Whitehead, M. (1999). *Supporting language and literacy development in the early years.* Buckingham: Open University Press.

Whitehead, M. (2002). Dylan's routes to literacy: The first three years with picture books. *Journal of Early Childhood Literacy, 2(3),* 269-290.

Whitehouse, M., & Colvin, C. (2001). Reading families: Deficit discourse and family literacy. *Theory into Practice, 430* 212-219.

Winter, P., & Rouse, J. (1990). Fostering intergenerational literacy: The Missouri parents as teachers program. *The Reading Teacher, 24(2),* 382-386.

Yaden, D.B. (Jr.), & Paratore, J.R. (2003). Family literacy at the turn of the millennium: The costly future of maintaining the status quo. In J. Flood, D. Lapp, J. Squire, & J. Jensen (Eds.). *Handbook of research on teaching the English language arts* (2nd ed.) (pp. 532-545). Mahwah, NJ: Lawrence Erlbaum Associates.

Yberra, L. (1999). The family/la familia. In E.J. Olmos, L. Yberra, & M. Monterrey (Eds.), *Americanos: Latino life in the United States/La vida Latino en los Estados Unidos* (p. 84). New York: Little, Brown & Company.

Index

Aboriginal 63, 70, 71, 90
Adult basic education 23, 26
Adult component 31, 33, 34, 35, 36, 94, 95
Adult literacy 19, 23, 26, 36, 40, 124, 126
Adult literacy materials 40
Advice and guidance 33
Alphabet 15, 41, 45, 52, 53, 55, 57, 86, 102, 105
Anecdotal reports 23, 87
Attention 13, 15, 17, 42, 79, 80, 81, 83, 87, 90, 95, 98, 101, 103, 109, 113, 120, 122
Attention Deficit Hyperactivity Disorder 15

Background knowledge 83
Basic Skills Agency 21, 29
Beginning with books 32, 33, 39
Better life 28, 121
Biological development 13
Book handling 41, 46
Book knowledge 37
Book sharing 20, 35
Books 32, 34, 35, 36, 38, 39, 47, 48, 49, 85, 86, 91, 94, 97, 98, 99, 102, 103, 105, 107, 108, 109, 111, 112, 114, 116, 117, 118, 119, 121
Book world 26
Bullying 116

Canadian Adult Reading Assessment 46

Caregiver 63
Case studies 25
Centre for Family Literacy 12, 29, 43
Child development 37, 93
Childcare 13, 20
Children's books 38, 85, 91, 98, 99
Circle time 36, 49, 78, 83, 85, 86
Classroom atmosphere 77, 78
Cognitive language and literacy development 16
Collaboration 12, 19, 20, 31, 79, 110
Coloring 78, 95, 98, 109, 116
Community groups 42
Community of learners 79
Community programs 10, 47, 48, 103, 110, 111, 122
Connected discourse 15
Context clues 83
Contextual variation 15
Control group 12, 21, 22, 43, 44, 48, 51, 52, 53, 55, 72, 73, 74, 76, 77, 115, 121, 122
Convention 45, 52, 53, 55, 56
Craft table 80, 81
Creative play 32, 33, 39
Cultural differences 20, 126
Cultural practice 24
Curriculum 18, 19, 30, 31, 32, 39, 40, 42, 85, 86

Daily activities 24
Decoding and comprehension skills 16
Decontextualized print 17, 28

Demographic data 63
Developing language for literacy 32, 34, 39, 78
Directed activities 36
Discipline 79, 94, 104, 114, 115
Distractions 83
Diversity 16, 20, 28

Early childhood education 23
Early literacy 31, 39, 42, 45
Early school leaving 92
Early years component 33, 34, 35, 36
Educational level 69, 70, 124
Emergent literacy 15, 16, 18, 19, 31, 125
Emotional development 15, 16
Employment status 21, 63, 66
Environmental print 18, 32, 33, 41, 85, 98
ESL (English as a Second Language) 83
Ethnicity 11, 12, 47, 63, 64, 69, 70, 71, 124
Even Start 20, 21
Evidence-based research 40
Expectations 11, 92, 121

Family circumstances 92, 106, 121, 122
Family instability 15
Family literacy 16, 17, 18, 19, 20, 21, 22, 23, 24, 25, 27, 28, 29, 30, 31, 37, 38, 41, 43, 124, 125, 126
Family literacy facilitators 20
Family literacy intervention programs 13
Family Literacy Works 21, 22, 23, 29, 31
Family storytelling 34
Favorite books 35, 36, 91, 102, 103, 119
Feedback 20, 29
Fetal alcohol spectrum disorder 15
Finger plays 34, 86
First language 47, 67, 70, 69
Formal literacies 27

Formal literacy experiences 17, 28
Formal literacy instruction 37, 121
Free play 36
Friends 90, 92, 94, 109, 114, 116, 117, 119
Frustration 78, 82

Games 33, 34, 39, 85, 86, 91, 101, 103, 104, 116, 118
Gender 12, 27, 47
General knowledge 15
Graded passages 46
Grammar 36

Head Start 20
Health 13, 20, 26, 42, 44
Home environment 15, 16
Home literacy 13, 17, 22, 25, 31, 97, 98
Home reading program 109, 112, 118, 121
Homelessness 15
Homework 104, 109 111, 112, 114

Illiteracy 21, 26
Imagination 34
Immigrant 37
Inequalities 11,12
Informal literacy experiences 17
Informal reading inventory 46
Interactions 15, 16, 20, 23, 27, 36, 40, 84, 86, 97, 108, 109
Interactive models 72, 74, 75
Intergenerational initiatives 19
Interpersonal violence 15
Intervention group 51, 52, 53, 55, 57, 72, 73, 74, 77, 115, 119
Interviewing 25

Joint interaction time 36
Joint sessions 21, 30, 31, 36, 37, 48, 49, 78, 79, 83, 84, 85, 96, 97
Journals 49, 107

Knowledge gap 38

Language development 15, 16, 79

Language facilitation 20
Language knowledge 17
Learning environment 38, 40, 79, 111
Learning Together 38, 40, 42, 43, 44, 47, 48, 79, 84, 85, 87, 88, 92, 94, 102, 103, 107, 109, 110, 111, 112, 114, 115, 121, 123, 124, 125, 126
Letters 17, 37, 41, 46, 49, 53, 82, 86, 91, 93, 95, 96, 98, 101, 102, 103, 105, 106, 114, 116, 117
Library skills 36
Life cycles education policy 26
Literacy development 12, 13, 14, 15, 16, 18, 19, 22, 23, 31, 34, 38, 39, 42, 86, 91, 108
Literacy events 37, 98, 100, 101
Literacy materials 40, 86, 98
Literacy spaces 102
Local literacies 26, 27
Loneliness 93
Longitudinal studies 19
Low income 23, 25, 37, 38
Low literacy 23, 25

Marital status 47, 63, 65
Meaning 52, 53, 55, 57, 58
Modeling 84, 98, 119
Motor development 15
Multiple measures 25

Non-literacy needs 44

Observation 25, 50, 82
Oral langue 17, 38, 39, 40, 42, 86

Parent interviews 12
Parent journal 79
Parent-child activities 20
Parent-child dyads 49, 78, 82
Parent-child engagement 79
Parenting 16, 21, 23, 26, 27, 44, 93
Passive role 118
Peabody Picture Vocabulary Test 22, 45
Personal values 18
Phonological awareness 15, 16

Physical well-being 15
Pilot study 29, 41
Policy implications 123
Political factors 17
Post-interviews 48
Post-school experiences 47
Poverty 14, 15, 21, 89, 27, 38
Preschool experiences 25
Preschool letter and phonological awareness 16
Preschool literacy 18
Pretest interview 47, 48
Print 16, 17, 18, 20, 27, 28, 32, 33, 34, 39, 41, 42, 45, 46, 85, 86, 91, 96, 97, 98, 99, 100, 102, 108, 114, 117, 118, 121, 125
Print conventions 46
printing 95, 120
Public library 114, 116, 118
Puppets 34

Questioning 20

Race 11, 27
Randomized control 25
Reading comprehension 36
Reading difficulties 16
Reading fluency 36
Receptive vocabulary 41
Reciprocal effects 25
Recruitment 24, 43, 44
Religious texts 91
Rereading books 97
Retention 24, 43
Rhymes 34, 49, 85, 86, 96
Risk-taking 79
Rural setting 30

Scaffolding 77, 79, 82
School achievement 25, 46
School experiences 47, 89, 92, 110, 115
School life 106, 112
School-centred view 18
Second language learners 88
Self-regulation 39
Shared book reading 17

Siblings 89, 108, 110, 117
Snack time 36, 49, 85
Social aspect of learning 95
Social benefits 26
Social competence 15
Social development 39
Social reform 14
Social response 95
Songs 14, 49, 86, 91, 96, 101, 103, 104, 116
Sound-letter correspondence 45
Specific language impairment 16
Spelling 36, 46, 104, 107, 108, 109, 110, 114, 120
Starting gate 11, 12
Story time 36, 111
Storytelling 74, 86
Strategies 17, 18, 20, 37, 43, 79, 82, 83, 95, 97, 98, 105, 118, 122, 125
Substance abuse 15, 44

Test of Early Reading Ability 45, 52

Unidimensional programs 14
Upgrading classes 107

Variety of print materials 37
Verbal ability 45
Vocabulary 15, 17, 22, 25, 38, 41, 45, 46
Wordless books 34
Words 18, 38, 39, 40, 46, 53, 79, 82, 83, 84, 86, 91, 93, 95, 96, 99, 101, 102, 104, 105, 106, 108, 115, 116, 118, 120
World of print 20
Writing 15, 18, 22, 32, 33, 38, 39, 47, 48, 49, 81, 83, 84, 85, 86, 91, 93, 95, 98, 99, 100, 101, 102, 104, 105, 106, 107, 108, 109, 111, 112, 112, 114, 116, 117, 118, 119, 120, 121
Writing ability 104
Writing and drawing 32, 39, 81, 102
Written registers 17